THE BLUEPRINT TO LIVE A LONGER, HEALTHIER LIFE

ELO MARC

CHAPTER 1
THE VISION OF LONGEVITY

Living longer isn't just about adding years to your life—it's about adding life to your years. While modern medicine has extended our lifespan, the quality of those extra years often leaves much to be desired. Longevity is not only about surviving but thriving, embracing vitality, and cherishing every moment.

To embark on the journey of living a longer, healthier life, we must understand two essential concepts: **healthspan** and **lifespan**.

Defining Healthspan vs. Lifespan

• **Lifespan** refers to the total number of years a person lives. It is determined by factors like genetics, environment, and medical advancements. Lifespan is the quantity of life.

• **Healthspan**, on the other hand, refers to the number of years one lives in good health, free from chronic diseases, pain, and disability. It is the quality of life.

While extending lifespan is an admirable goal, it becomes truly meaningful only when paired with an extended healthspan. A long life without the ability to enjoy it—filled with illness, dependency, or suffering—is far from ideal. This book focuses on strategies to maximize your healthspan, allowing you to thrive throughout your entire life.

The Pillars of Living a Long, Fulfilling Life

The journey to a longer, healthier life rests on **five core pillars**:

1 Nutrition

◦ What you eat directly impacts your energy, cellular health, and resilience against disease. A diet rich in whole, nutrient-dense foods lays the foundation for longevity.

2 Movement

◦ Staying active is essential for maintaining strength, flexibility, and cardiovascular health. Exercise also protects mental health and cognitive function.

3 Restoration

◦ Sleep and relaxation are when your body repairs itself. Proper rest rejuvenates your mind and body, preparing you for the challenges of tomorrow.

4 Social Connections

◦ Humans are wired for connection. Deep, meaningful relationships and a sense of community significantly enhance mental and physical well-being.

5 Purpose and Mindset

◦ A sense of purpose gives life meaning and direction. Coupled with a positive outlook, it boosts resilience and helps you navigate life's inevitable ups and downs.

The Path Ahead

Throughout this book, you'll explore evidence-based strategies to strengthen each of these pillars. You'll learn to make sustainable changes that align with your unique lifestyle, preferences, and goals.

The vision of longevity is not about perfection but about creating a balance that works for you—a blueprint for living longer and healthier, one step at a time. Together, we'll uncover how small, consistent actions can lead to profound transformations.

Are you ready to embrace your blueprint for a vibrant, fulfilling life? Let's begin.

CHAPTER 2

UNDERSTANDING THE BLUEPRINT

Every great endeavor begins with a clear plan. To unlock the secrets of a longer, healthier life, you need a blueprint—a practical, adaptable framework based on the wisdom of science, tradition, and real-world examples. This chapter introduces the key principles that will guide your journey and explores the lessons we can learn from those who have lived long, vibrant lives: the centenarians.

Key Principles of Longevity

1 Nutrition:

◦ The food you eat serves as the fuel and building blocks for your body. Every bite either promotes vitality or accelerates aging.

◦ Prioritize a diet rich in natural, whole foods: vegetables, fruits, whole grains, legumes, nuts, and seeds. Limit processed foods, added sugars, and unhealthy fats.

◦ Timing matters—adopting practices like time-restricted eating or intermittent fasting can support cellular repair and metabolic health.

2 Lifestyle:

◦ Longevity is a lifestyle, not a temporary fix. Small, consistent actions compound over time to yield significant benefits.

◦ Movement is essential: daily physical activity keeps your muscles strong, your heart healthy, and your mind sharp.

◦ Restoration through quality sleep and stress management is just as vital. Allow your body and mind time to recover, rejuvenate, and grow.

3 Mindset:

◦ A positive and resilient mindset forms the foundation for a fulfilling life. Optimism, gratitude, and emotional flexibility can help you navigate life's challenges.

◦ Cultivate a sense of purpose (Ikigai) to add meaning to your daily life. A strong sense of why can sustain you through anything.

Learning from Centenarians

Centenarians—those who live to 100 years or more—offer invaluable insights into the art of longevity. Studies of these individuals in **Blue Zones** (regions with exceptionally high rates of centenarians) reveal common traits and practices that contribute to their remarkable health and vitality.

1 Diet and Eating Habits:

◦ Centenarians typically follow plant-based diets rich in legumes, vegetables, and whole grains, with minimal processed foods or red meat.

◦ They eat mindfully, often stopping when 80% full, a practice known as *hara hachi bu* in Okinawa, Japan.

2 Active Lifestyles:

◦ Physical activity is integrated naturally into their daily routines, such as gardening, walking, or manual labor. It's not about gym workouts but consistent movement.

3 Strong Social Connections:

◦ Centenarians often live in close-knit communities where relationships are prioritized. Regular interaction with family, friends, and neighbors provides emotional support and reduces stress.

4 Purposeful Living:

◦ A sense of purpose—whether caring for family, practicing a craft, or contributing to the community—keeps their minds and spirits engaged.

5 Stress Reduction and Balance:

◦ They practice relaxation techniques, whether through prayer, meditation, or spending time in nature. These activities lower stress and promote inner peace.

Applying the Blueprint

The longevity blueprint isn't about adopting rigid rules or mimicking others—it's about identifying principles that resonate with you and tailoring them to fit your unique life. By combining the wisdom of centenarians with modern science, you can create a sustainable, personalized path toward a longer, healthier, and more fulfilling life.

Are you ready to embrace this journey and start building your blueprint? With the foundation set, let's dive deeper into each element and transform your vision of longevity into reality.

CHAPTER 3

THE POWER OF PURPOSE

THE ROLE OF IKIGAI (REASON FOR BEING)

In the pursuit of a long, healthy life, **purpose** plays an essential role. It's the force that drives us to get out of bed in the morning, to face challenges with resilience, and to keep striving toward our goals. But not all purposes are created equal. Some are fleeting or external, while others are deeply rooted in our own identity and passions.

One of the most profound concepts related to purpose comes from Japan, where it is called **Ikigai**. Ikigai is often translated as "a reason for being"—the intersection of four essential elements:

1. What you love

2. What you're good at

3. What the world needs

4. What you can be paid for (if applicable)

When these four elements align, you experience a deep sense of fulfillment and meaning. This harmony leads to a stronger sense of purpose and, ultimately, longevity. People who find their Ikigai tend to live longer lives, as their daily activities are infused with meaning, contributing to emotional and physical well-being.

How Purpose Adds Years to Life

Numerous studies support the connection between having a purpose and living a longer, healthier life. People with a clear sense of purpose tend to live with greater intention, which has a profound impact on both mental and physical health. Here's how purpose directly influences longevity:

1.**Stress Reduction**:

Having a purpose helps buffer the negative effects of stress. When you have a clear reason for living, you are more likely to approach life's challenges with a positive outlook. Purpose gives you perspective, helping you cope with adversity in healthier ways.

2.**Increased Resilience**:

People with a purpose are more resilient in the face of illness or setbacks. They are more likely to engage in healthy behaviors, maintain social connections, and push through difficult times. The drive to fulfill their purpose gives them the strength to overcome obstacles.

3.**Lower Risk of Disease**:

Research has shown that those who report a strong sense of purpose experience lower levels of inflammation, reduced risk of heart disease, and improved immune function. This is likely due to the stress-reducing and health-boosting effects of having a clear, motivating reason for living.

4.**Improved Mental Health**:

A strong sense of purpose has been linked to a decreased risk of depression and anxiety. People with purpose are more likely to have positive emotions, feel a sense of satisfaction, and experience fewer feelings of loneliness or isolation.

5.**Better Sleep and Physical Activity**:

Purpose-driven individuals are often more active and sleep better. When you have a reason to get up in the morning, you're more likely to engage in healthy habits—such as physical activity, healthy eating, and regular sleep—each of which contributes to overall longevity.

Finding and Cultivating Your Ikigai

While finding your Ikigai can be a lifelong journey, it's never too late to begin. Here are steps to help uncover your purpose and integrate it into your daily life:

1.**Self-Reflection:**

Take time to reflect on your passions, talents, and values. What activities make you feel most alive? What skills or strengths do you bring to the world?

2.**Identify What the World Needs**:

Think about how your unique abilities can benefit others or the larger community. Purpose often comes from making a positive impact, whether small or large.

3.**Align With Your Values**:

Identify what truly matters to you. Is it helping others? Creating art? Solving problems? Having a clear understanding of your core values will make it easier to find purpose.

4.**Experiment and Adapt:**

Sometimes finding purpose takes experimentation. Pursue new hobbies, engage in different activities, or take on projects that align with your passions. Purpose often evolves, and it's important to stay flexible and open to change.

5.**Connect With Others:**

Surround yourself with people who share your interests or inspire you. Meaningful relationships can support your journey and help you stay grounded in your purpose.

Purpose in Action: Lessons from Centenarians

Centenarians in Blue Zones—places known for high rates of people living to 100—often credit their longevity to a deep sense of purpose. For example:

• **Okinawa, Japan**: *Residents follow the concept of Ikigai, where each person is committed to a specific role or passion that brings meaning to their life, whether through family, work, or community involvement.*

• **Sardinia, Italy**: *Many centenarians in Sardinia find purpose in family and community. Their days are filled with shared meals, farming, and taking care of grandchildren. Their purpose is deeply intertwined with their roles within the family and the community.*

• **Nicoya Peninsula, Costa Rica**: *People in Nicoya often attribute their long lives to their sense of purpose, which includes work and family responsibilities. Their daily routines are filled with tasks they find meaningful, whether it's caring for land or providing for loved ones.*

Purpose is more than just a psychological benefit—it's a biological advantage. The power of purpose isn't just in the sense of accomplishment or fulfillment; it physically impacts your health, strengthens your relationships, and propels you to live a longer, more vibrant life.

By aligning your actions with your deepest values and passions, you can unlock your own Ikigai and experience the profound benefits of living with purpose. Whether through work, relationships, hobbies, or service, your purpose can guide you toward a life of meaning, vitality, and longevity.

CHAPTER 4
STRESS MANAGEMENT FOR THE AGES
UNDERSTANDING STRESS'S IMPACT ON AGING

Stress is a silent accelerant of aging, with effects that extend beyond the psychological to deeply impact physical health. When faced with stress, the body activates the **fight-or-flight response**, releasing hormones such as cortisol and adrenaline. While this response is helpful in short-term emergencies, chronic stress creates a state of constant arousal that wreaks havoc on the body over time.

Key Effects of Chronic Stress on Aging:

1.**Cellular Aging:**

◦ *Stress shortens* **telomeres**, *the protective caps at the ends of chromosomes. As telomeres shrink, cells lose their ability to divide and regenerate, accelerating aging.*

2.**Inflammation:**

◦ *Prolonged stress leads to chronic inflammation, a driver of many age-related diseases, including heart disease, arthritis, and diabetes.*

3.**Brain Health:**

○ *Persistent stress impairs memory and cognitive function by damaging the hippocampus, the brain's memory center. This increases the risk of neurodegenerative diseases like Alzheimer's.*

4.Weakened Immunity:

○ *Stress suppresses the immune system, making the body more susceptible to infections and slowing down the healing process.*

5.Emotional Health:

○ *Chronic stress contributes to anxiety, depression, and sleep disorders, all of which further exacerbate physical decline.*

Understanding these impacts underscores why managing stress is essential for longevity and overall health.

Practical Techniques: Mindfulness, Meditation, and Breathwork

Effectively managing stress can reverse many of its harmful effects and slow the aging process. These techniques offer scientifically-backed methods to calm the mind and body, promoting resilience and inner peace.

Mindfulness: Living in the Present

What It Is:

Mindfulness involves paying attention to the present moment without judgment. By focusing on "now," you disengage from the mental loops of past regrets and future worries that amplify stress.

Benefits:

• *Reduces cortisol levels*

• *Improves emotional regulation*

• *Enhances focus and mental clarity*

How to Practice:

• **Mindful Breathing**: *Spend a few minutes observing your breath, noting the sensations of air entering and leaving your body.*

• **Body Scan**: *Slowly bring attention to each part of your body, starting from your toes and moving upward, noting any sensations without trying to change them.*

• **Mindful Walking**: *Focus on the rhythm of your steps, the feel of the ground beneath your feet, and the sights and sounds around you.*

Meditation: Cultivating Inner Calm

What It Is:

Meditation is the practice of focusing your mind to achieve a state of relaxation and heightened awareness. Regular meditation strengthens your brain's ability to manage stress and promotes a sense of peace.

Benefits:

• *Lowers blood pressure and heart rate*

• *Improves emotional resilience*

• *Enhances creativity and problem-solving*

How to Practice:

• **Guided Meditation**: *Use apps like Calm or Headspace to follow a structured meditation session.*

• **Mantra Meditation**: *Silently repeat a calming word or phrase, like "peace" or "calm," to center your thoughts.*

• **Loving-Kindness Meditation**: *Focus on sending positive thoughts and well-wishes to yourself and others, fostering compassion and connection.*

Breathwork: Harnessing the Power of Breath

What It Is:

Breathwork is the intentional control of breathing patterns to influence mental, emotional, and physical states. Deep, controlled breathing activates the **parasympathetic nervous system**, reducing stress and promoting relaxation.

Benefits:

- *Lowers cortisol and stress hormone levels*

- *Improves oxygen delivery to the brain and body*

- *Enhances emotional regulation*

How to Practice:

1. Box Breathing: *Inhale for 4 counts, hold for 4 counts, exhale for 4 counts, and hold again for 4 counts. Repeat for several cycles.*

2. 4-7-8 Technique: *Inhale for 4 counts, hold for 7 counts, and exhale slowly for 8 counts. This technique is especially effective before sleep.*

3. Diaphragmatic Breathing: *Breathe deeply into your diaphragm, ensuring your stomach rises and falls with each breath. This reduces shallow chest breathing often associated with stress.*

Putting It All Together

Incorporating mindfulness, meditation, and breathwork into your daily routine doesn't require a significant time investment. Even 10-15 minutes a day can yield remarkable results.

Sample Routine for Stress Relief:

1. Morning: *Begin the day with a 5-minute meditation to set a positive tone.*

2. Afternoon: *Take a 10-minute mindful walk during lunch to reset your mind.*

3. Evening: *Practice 4-7-8 breathing before bed to unwind and prepare for restful sleep.*

A Life of Balance

Stress is inevitable, but its effects on aging are not. By embracing tools like mindfulness, meditation, and breathwork, you can build a stress management toolkit that promotes longevity, vitality, and emotional balance. These practices not only enhance your healthspan but also enrich your quality of life, ensuring that each day is lived with greater calm and clarity.

Your body and mind will thank you—not just today but for decades to come.

CHAPTER 5
THE SCIENCE OF OPTIMISM
POSITIVE THINKING AND ITS LINK TO LONGEVITY

Optimism isn't just a mindset—it's a scientifically validated tool for living longer and healthier. Studies consistently show that positive thinking is closely tied to increased lifespan, better health outcomes, and improved resilience against age-related decline. Optimists tend to see challenges as opportunities, setbacks as temporary, and the future as bright. This mental outlook has profound effects on the body and mind.

How Optimism Influences Longevity:

1.Reduced Stress Levels:

Optimists are better at managing stress, which lowers levels of cortisol and reduces the risk of chronic inflammation, a major contributor to aging and disease.

2.Improved Heart Health:

Optimistic individuals have lower blood pressure and a reduced risk of cardiovascular disease. A positive outlook is associated with healthier lifestyle choices, such as exercising regularly and eating well.

3.Enhanced Immune Function:

Optimism boosts the immune system, making the body more effective at fighting infections and recovering from illness.

4.Resilience and Recovery:

Optimists recover faster from illnesses and surgeries. Their ability to focus on solutions and maintain hope contributes to better healing and reduced hospital stays.

5.Mental Well-being:

A positive outlook protects against depression and anxiety, common conditions that can shorten lifespan and diminish quality of life.

Cultivating Gratitude

Gratitude is a cornerstone of optimism and a proven pathway to greater happiness and longevity. It shifts focus from what is lacking to what is abundant, fostering a positive perspective on life. By practicing gratitude, individuals can rewire their brains to notice and appreciate the good in their lives, even during difficult times.

The Science Behind Gratitude and Health:

1.Boosts Emotional Health:

Grateful individuals experience more positive emotions, less anxiety, and greater satisfaction with life.

2.Improves Sleep:

Regularly reflecting on things you're thankful for before bed improves sleep quality and duration.

3.Enhances Physical Health:

Gratitude is associated with reduced inflammation, lower blood pressure, and a stronger immune system.

4.Strengthens Relationships:

Expressing gratitude strengthens social bonds, improves communication, and fosters a sense of belonging, all of which are vital for longevity.

Practical Ways to Cultivate Optimism and Gratitude

1. Reframe Challenges:

• *When facing difficulties, look for silver linings or lessons that can be learned. Ask yourself, "What can I gain from this experience?"*

2. Practice Daily Gratitude:

• *Keep a gratitude journal. Write down three things you're thankful for each day. These can be as simple as a warm meal or a kind gesture from a friend.*

• *Share gratitude with others. Tell loved ones how much you appreciate them—it strengthens relationships and uplifts both parties.*

3. Surround Yourself With Positivity:

• *Spend time with optimistic, supportive people. Positivity is contagious, and the right company can help you maintain a hopeful outlook.*

4. Visualize Success:

• *Use visualization techniques to imagine positive outcomes for your goals and challenges. This primes your mind for success and motivates you to take constructive action.*

5. Mindfulness and Meditation:

• *Practice mindfulness to focus on the present moment and reduce negative rumination.*

• *Gratitude meditations can help you develop a deep sense of appreciation for your life.*

6. Volunteer and Give Back:

• Helping others fosters a sense of purpose and gratitude. It reminds you of the impact you can have and shifts focus away from personal struggles.

Lessons From Optimists

Research on centenarians and people in Blue Zones—regions known for exceptional longevity—shows that a positive outlook on life is a common trait among those who live the longest.

• **Sardinia, Italy**: *Sardinians are known for their humor and lightheartedness. Laughing and staying connected to family and community contribute to their mental and emotional health.*

• **Okinawa, Japan**: *Okinawans practice moai, social groups that provide emotional support and foster a sense of belonging. This encourages optimism and reduces stress.*

• **Nicoya, Costa Rica**: *People in Nicoya are naturally optimistic and grateful for their strong family ties and sense of purpose, which contribute to their happiness and longevity.*

Optimism as a Longevity Tool

The science is clear: optimism and gratitude are powerful allies in the quest for a longer, healthier life. By shifting your mindset to focus on the positive and cultivating appreciation for what you have, you can reduce stress, improve health, and strengthen relationships. Optimism isn't just a natural trait—it's a skill that can be practiced and developed over time.

Embracing positivity doesn't mean ignoring life's challenges; rather, it's about choosing to focus on what uplifts and empowers you. By integrating optimism and gratitude into your daily life, you lay a strong foundation for resilience, happiness, and vitality that will carry you through the years with grace and fulfillment.

CHAPTER 6

THE FOUNDATIONS OF LONGEVITY EATING
WHOLE FOODS AND NUTRIENT DENSITY

What we eat profoundly affects how we age. The foundation of a longevity-focused diet is built on **whole, nutrient-dense foods** that nourish the body at a cellular level. These foods provide the essential vitamins, minerals, and antioxidants needed to support bodily functions, reduce inflammation, and repair cellular damage—key factors in slowing the aging process.

What Are Whole Foods?

Whole foods are minimally processed and as close as possible to their natural state. Examples include fresh fruits and vegetables, whole grains, nuts, seeds, legumes, and lean proteins. These foods are free from additives, preservatives, and artificial ingredients, making them superior sources of nutrition.

Nutrient Density Defined:

Nutrient-dense foods pack a high concentration of vitamins, minerals, and other beneficial compounds (like antioxidants and phytochemicals) relative to their calorie content. This means you get maximum nutrition with fewer calories—critical for maintaining energy and health while preventing weight gain as you age.

Key Benefits of Nutrient-Dense Whole Foods:

1.Reduced Inflammation:

Whole foods are rich in antioxidants, which neutralize free radicals and reduce oxidative stress, a major contributor to aging.

2.Improved Gut Health:

High-fiber whole foods support a diverse gut microbiome, essential for digestion, immunity, and even mental health.

3.Balanced Energy Levels:

Nutrient-dense foods provide sustained energy without the blood sugar spikes and crashes caused by processed foods.

4.Support for Brain Health:

Foods like leafy greens, berries, and omega-3-rich fish are packed with compounds that protect brain cells and improve cognitive function.

Why Processed Foods Accelerate Aging

Processed foods are the antithesis of a longevity diet. They are typically stripped of nutrients, loaded with unhealthy additives, and designed to be hyper-palatable, encouraging overeating. These foods are not only nutrient-poor but also harmful in several ways that accelerate the aging process.

Characteristics of Processed Foods:

- *High in refined sugars and unhealthy fats*

- *Low in fiber and essential nutrients*

- *Contain artificial preservatives, colorings, and flavorings*

- *Often calorie-dense but nutritionally empty*

How Processed Foods Impact Aging:

1.**Promote Chronic Inflammation:**

◦ *Processed foods are rich in refined sugars and omega-6 fatty acids, which can trigger systemic inflammation, a key driver of many age-related diseases.*

2.**Increase Oxidative Stress:**

◦ *Lack of antioxidants in processed foods means the body struggles to neutralize free radicals, leading to cellular damage and faster aging.*

3.**Damage to the Gut Microbiome:**

◦ *The low fiber content and high levels of artificial ingredients in processed foods disrupt the gut microbiome, weakening immunity and increasing inflammation.*

4.**Accelerate Cognitive Decline:**

◦ *Diets high in refined sugars and trans fats have been linked to memory impairments and an increased risk of neurodegenerative diseases like Alzheimer's.*

5.**Trigger Insulin Resistance:**

◦ *Consuming excessive refined carbohydrates leads to frequent blood sugar spikes and insulin resistance, contributing to diabetes, weight gain, and premature aging.*

Principles of Longevity Eating

To eat for longevity, focus on incorporating whole foods into every meal and reducing your reliance on processed and packaged foods.

1.**Prioritize Plants:**

◦ **Fruits and Vegetables**: *Aim for a variety of colors to maximize your intake of antioxidants and phytochemicals.*

◦ **Whole Grains**: *Replace refined grains with nutrient-dense options like quinoa, farro, and oats.*

2.Include Healthy Fats:

◦ *Opt for fats from whole foods, such as avocados, nuts, seeds, and fatty fish. Avoid trans fats and heavily processed oils.*

3.Choose Quality Protein:

◦ *Include plant-based proteins like beans, lentils, and tofu alongside lean animal proteins like fish, poultry, and eggs.*

4.Hydrate with Purpose:

◦ *Drink water, herbal teas, and other unsweetened beverages. Avoid sugary drinks and artificial sweeteners, which can disrupt metabolism and gut health.*

5.Minimize Added Sugars:

◦ *Reduce your intake of added sugars, which are found in sodas, desserts, and many packaged foods. Use natural sweeteners sparingly, like honey or dates.*

How to Transition to a Longevity Diet

1.Start Small:

◦ *Gradually replace processed snacks with whole-food alternatives, such as swapping chips for nuts or fresh fruit.*

2.Cook at Home:

◦ *Prepare meals from scratch to control ingredients and avoid hidden additives.*

3.Read Labels:

◦ *Choose products with minimal, recognizable ingredients and avoid those with long lists of additives.*

4.Plan Balanced Meals:

◦ *Build meals around a base of vegetables, complemented by whole grains, lean proteins, and healthy fats.*

5.Batch Cook:

○ *Prepare large portions of whole-food meals in advance to make it easier to eat healthy during busy days.*

Building the Foundation for a Longer Life

Longevity begins with what you put on your plate. By prioritizing whole, nutrient-dense foods and reducing your intake of processed options, you empower your body to age gracefully and maintain vitality. Nutrition isn't just about calories—it's about providing the building blocks your body needs to thrive over time.

In the chapters to come, we'll explore specific foods, meal plans, and dietary strategies that align with the principles of longevity eating, helping you craft a lifestyle that supports both a longer life and a richer, healthier experience along the way.

CHAPTER 7

THE POWER OF PLANT-BASED EATING

THE BENEFITS OF FRUITS, VEGETABLES, LEGUMES, AND WHOLE GRAINS

Plant-based eating is one of the most effective dietary approaches for promoting longevity. A diet rich in fruits, vegetables, legumes, and whole grains provides the body with essential nutrients, antioxidants, and fiber while reducing the risks associated with chronic diseases. Whether you fully adopt a plant-based diet or simply include more plant-focused meals in your routine, the benefits are undeniable.

Why Plant-Based Eating Works for Longevity:

1.Rich in Antioxidants:

◦ *Fruits and vegetables are abundant in antioxidants, which combat oxidative stress and neutralize free radicals, reducing cellular damage and slowing aging.*

2.High in Fiber:

◦ *Whole grains, legumes, and vegetables provide soluble and insoluble fiber, which promotes healthy digestion, supports the gut microbiome, and lowers cholesterol levels.*

3.Anti-Inflammatory Properties:

◦ *Many plant-based foods, such as leafy greens, berries, and nuts, have natural anti-inflammatory compounds that protect against heart disease, arthritis, and other age-related conditions.*

4.Reduced Risk of Chronic Diseases:

◦ *Plant-based diets are associated with lower rates of heart disease, type 2 diabetes, obesity, and certain cancers, all of which can shorten lifespan.*

5.Improved Weight Management:

◦ *Plant-based foods are nutrient-dense but lower in calories, helping maintain a healthy weight and reducing the risk of metabolic disorders.*

Key Plant-Based Food Groups for Longevity:

·Fruits and Vegetables:

These are the cornerstone of plant-based diets, providing essential vitamins, minerals, and antioxidants. Aim to "eat the rainbow" by incorporating a wide variety of colors to ensure a broad spectrum of nutrients.

·Legumes:

Beans, lentils, and chickpeas are high in protein, fiber, and iron. They are a staple in many long-lived populations, providing energy and promoting satiety.

·Whole Grains:

Brown rice, quinoa, oats, and barley are rich in fiber and B vitamins, supporting heart health, digestion, and energy levels.

·Nuts and Seeds:

Almonds, walnuts, chia seeds, and flaxseeds are excellent sources of healthy fats, protein, and omega-3 fatty acids, which are crucial for brain and heart health.

Blue Zone Dietary Insights

The Blue Zones are regions of the world where people live longer, healthier lives, often exceeding 100 years of age. These areas include Sardinia (Italy), Okinawa (Japan), Nicoya (Costa Rica), Ikaria (Greece), and the Seventh-day Adventist community in Loma Linda (California). A common thread among these populations is their predominantly plant-based diets.

What We Can Learn From the Blue Zones:

1.75-95% Plant-Based Diets:

○ *Blue Zone diets consist primarily of plants, with animal products consumed sparingly or as a side dish.*

2.Daily Legume Consumption:

○ *Beans, lentils, and chickpeas are daily staples, providing high-quality protein, fiber, and nutrients.*

3.Whole Foods Over Processed:

○ *Blue Zone residents avoid processed and refined foods, focusing instead on whole, natural ingredients.*

4.Portion Control and Eating Habits:

○ *In Okinawa, the concept of hara hachi bu (eating until 80% full) is practiced, which helps prevent overeating and promotes better digestion.*

5.Seasonal and Local Eating:

○ *Blue Zone diets rely on fresh, seasonal, and locally sourced produce, ensuring maximum nutrient density and minimal environmental impact.*

6.Healthy Fats from Plants:

○ *Nuts, seeds, olive oil, and avocados are preferred sources of fat, reducing reliance on saturated fats from animal products.*

Practical Tips for Incorporating More Plants into Your Diet

1.Start With One Plant-Based Meal a Day:

◦ *Replace one meal, such as breakfast or lunch, with a plant-based option. Try oatmeal with fruit or a quinoa salad with roasted vegetables.*

2.Make Plants the Star of Your Plate:

◦ *Shift your focus from meat-centered meals to vegetable-forward dishes. Use animal protein as a garnish rather than the main component.*

3.Experiment With Legumes:

◦ *Add beans or lentils to soups, stews, salads, and even desserts like black bean brownies.*

4.Snack Smart:

◦ *Replace processed snacks with raw veggies, hummus, fresh fruit, or a handful of nuts.*

5.Cook More at Home:

◦ *Preparing your own meals allows you to experiment with plant-based recipes and control the quality of ingredients.*

6.Blend and Juice:

◦ *Smoothies and fresh juices are an easy way to pack a variety of fruits and vegetables into your diet.*

Sample Longevity Plate

• **Main Dish:** *Quinoa and black bean bowl with sautéed spinach, roasted sweet potatoes, and avocado slices.*

• **Side:** *A mixed green salad with cherry tomatoes, cucumbers, and a lemon-tahini dressing.*

• **Dessert:** *Fresh berries with a dollop of coconut yogurt.*

• **Drink:** *Herbal tea or water infused with cucumber and mint.*

A Plant-Powered Path to Longevity

Plant-based eating isn't just a diet—it's a lifestyle that prioritizes health, vitality, and sustainability. By focusing on fruits, vegetables, legumes, and whole grains, you can lower your risk of chronic diseases, enhance your overall well-being, and create a foundation for a long and vibrant life.

The Blue Zones show us that plant-based diets are not only achievable but also delicious and deeply rewarding. Start small, explore new recipes, and celebrate the power of plants to transform your health and your future.

CHAPTER 8
HEALTHY FATS FOR A HEALTHY LIFE
THE IMPORTANCE OF HEALTHY FATS

Fats often get a bad reputation, but they're essential for health and longevity. The key is choosing the right types of fats—those that nourish the body and support critical functions like brain health, heart health, and hormonal balance. Incorporating healthy fats into your diet is a cornerstone of a longevity-focused lifestyle, while avoiding harmful fats can significantly reduce the risk of chronic diseases.

Healthy Fats: The Heroes of Longevity

1. Omega-3 Fatty Acids

Omega-3 fatty acids are essential fats that the body cannot produce on its own, so they must be obtained from food. These fats are known for their anti-inflammatory properties and their ability to protect against heart disease, cognitive decline, and arthritis.

Sources of Omega-3s:

• **Fatty Fish:** *Salmon, mackerel, sardines, and trout are rich in EPA and DHA, the most bioavailable forms of omega-3s.*

• **Plant-Based Sources:** *Flaxseeds, chia seeds, walnuts, and hemp seeds* *provide ALA, which the body can convert into EPA and DHA (though less efficiently).*

• **Algal Oil:** *A vegan-friendly supplement derived from algae that provides EPA and DHA.*

Benefits of Omega-3s:

• *Lower blood pressure and reduce triglyceride levels*

• *Improve brain function and reduce the risk of Alzheimer's disease*

• *Combat inflammation, which is linked to aging and chronic diseases*

2. Nuts and Seeds

Nuts and seeds are small but mighty sources of healthy fats, protein, fiber, and essential nutrients. They are a staple in longevity diets, such as those followed in Blue Zones.

Best Nuts and Seeds for Longevity:

• **Almonds:** *High in monounsaturated fats and vitamin E, which supports skin and heart health.*

• **Walnuts:** *Rich in omega-3s and antioxidants that promote brain and heart health.*

• **Chia and Flaxseeds:** *Packed with fiber, omega-3s, and lignans, which have anti-inflammatory and cancer-fighting properties.*

• **Pumpkin Seeds:** *A great source of magnesium, zinc, and healthy fats for overall health.*

How to Incorporate Nuts and Seeds:

• *Add them to oatmeal, salads, or yogurt.*

• *Blend them into smoothies or use them to make homemade nut butters.*

• *Snack on a small handful for a quick energy boost.*

3. Avocados

Avocados are a unique fruit packed with heart-healthy monounsaturated fats, fiber, and a variety of vitamins and minerals. They are a delicious and versatile addition to any longevity diet.

Why Avocados Are Beneficial:

• *Promote heart health by reducing LDL (bad) cholesterol and increasing HDL (good) cholesterol.*

• *Support brain health with their high content of monounsaturated fats and vitamin E.*

• *Aid in digestion and weight management due to their fiber content.*

Ways to Enjoy Avocados:

• *Spread on whole-grain toast with a sprinkle of seeds.*

• *Add to salads, sandwiches, or smoothies.*

• *Use as a base for guacamole or creamy dressings.*

Unhealthy Fats: The Villains of Longevity

1. Trans Fats

Trans fats are artificially created fats found in partially hydrogenated oils, commonly used in processed and fried foods. They are harmful and have no safe level of consumption.

Foods High in Trans Fats:

• *Packaged snacks like cookies, crackers, and chips*

• *Fried fast foods*

• *Margarine and shortening*

Health Risks of Trans Fats:

• *Increase LDL (bad) cholesterol and decrease HDL (good) cholesterol*

• *Raise the risk of heart disease, stroke, and type 2 diabetes*

• *Promote inflammation and contribute to aging*

2. Refined and Hydrogenated Oils

Refined oils, such as soybean, canola, and corn oil, are often heavily processed and stripped of nutrients. These oils can be high in omega-6 fatty acids, which, when consumed in excess, may contribute to inflammation.

Alternatives to Refined Oils:

• *Use* **extra virgin olive oil** *for cooking and dressings.*

• *Opt for* **avocado oil** *for high-heat cooking.*

• *Choose* **coconut oil** *in moderation for baking and specific recipes.*

Practical Tips for Incorporating Healthy Fats

1.Replace Bad Fats with Good Fats:

◦ *Swap margarine and shortening for olive oil or avocado oil.*

◦ *Replace processed snacks with nuts or seeds.*

2.Moderation is Key:

◦ *While healthy fats are beneficial, they are calorie-dense. Stick to appropriate portions, such as a handful of nuts or half an avocado per serving.*

3.Prioritize Whole Food Sources:

◦ *Get your fats from whole foods like fish, nuts, seeds, and avocados rather than relying on processed oils.*

4.Be Mindful of Cooking Methods:

◦ *Avoid deep-frying and instead use steaming, baking, or sautéing with healthy oils.*

5.Read Labels Carefully:

◦ *Look for hidden trans fats and refined oils in packaged foods. If you see "partially hydrogenated" on the label, avoid it.*

Fats That Fuel Longevity

Healthy fats are essential to a balanced diet and play a pivotal role in promoting a longer, healthier life. From the brain-boosting power of omega-3s to the heart-friendly benefits of avocados, nuts, and seeds, incorporating these fats into your daily meals can enhance your healthspan and overall vitality.

By avoiding trans fats and refined oils and focusing on nutrient-rich, unprocessed sources of fats, you can protect your heart, sharpen your mind, and support your body's natural aging processes. Fats are not the enemy—in fact, they may be your greatest ally in the journey toward longevity.

CHAPTER 9

THE PROTEIN PUZZLE

Protein is a vital macronutrient that serves as the building block for muscles, tissues, enzymes, and hormones. For those pursuing a long and healthy life, the type, amount, and source of protein play a critical role. Striking the right balance between animal and plant-based protein can help maintain muscle mass, support bodily functions, and reduce the risk of chronic diseases as we age.

The Role of Protein in Longevity

Protein is essential for:

• **Muscle Maintenance:** *Prevents muscle loss (sarcopenia), which is common with aging.*

• **Cell Repair:** *Repairs damaged tissues and maintains cellular health.*

• **Enzyme and Hormone Production:** *Vital for digestion, metabolism, and overall bodily function.*

• **Immune Support:** *Builds antibodies and other immune system components.*

As we age, protein becomes even more important. After age 40, muscle mass begins to decline by about 1% per year, making adequate protein intake critical to maintain strength and mobility.

Animal vs. Plant-Based Protein

1. Animal Protein

Animal proteins are considered "complete proteins" because they contain all nine essential amino acids needed by the body. These sources include:

• *Meat (chicken, beef, pork, lamb)*

• *Fish and seafood*

• *Eggs*

• *Dairy products*

Benefits of Animal Protein:

• *High-quality protein for muscle synthesis and repair*

• *Rich in iron (heme iron), which is more easily absorbed than plant-based iron*

• *Good sources of vitamin B12, which supports brain and nervous system health*

Drawbacks of Animal Protein:

• *High consumption of red and processed meats is linked to increased risks of heart disease, cancer, and inflammation.*

• *Saturated fats in some animal proteins can contribute to cholesterol issues if consumed in excess.*

2. Plant-Based Protein

Plant-based proteins are derived from sources such as:

- *Legumes (beans, lentils, chickpeas)*

- *Nuts and seeds*

- *Whole grains (quinoa, oats, farro)*

- *Soy products (tofu, tempeh, edamame)*

While most plant-based proteins are "incomplete" (missing one or more essential amino acids), combining different sources can create a complete amino acid profile. For example:

- **Rice + Beans**

- **Hummus + Whole-Grain Pita**

Benefits of Plant-Based Protein:

- *Lower in saturated fat and cholesterol*

- *High in fiber, antioxidants, and phytonutrients, which reduce inflammation*

- *Linked to a reduced risk of chronic diseases like heart disease and type 2 diabetes*

Drawbacks of Plant-Based Protein:

- *Requires intentional pairing of foods to ensure complete amino acid intake.*

- *May require larger portions to meet protein needs compared to animal sources.*

Finding the Balance

Protein Needs for Longevity

·Daily Recommendations:

Adults should aim for 0.8–1.2 grams of protein per kilogram of body weight, with higher needs for older adults (1.2–1.6

grams/kg). For example, a 150-pound person (68 kg) would need approximately 82–109 grams of protein daily.

·Timing Matters:

Distribute protein intake evenly throughout the day to maximize muscle protein synthesis.

Balancing Animal and Plant Proteins

Striking a balance is key to reaping the benefits of both animal and plant-based proteins while minimizing potential drawbacks.

• **Aim for a 70/30 or 50/50 Ratio:** *Depending on your personal health goals and ethical preferences, incorporate both sources, with a focus on plant-based options.*

• **Prioritize Lean Animal Proteins:** *Choose chicken, fish, eggs, and low-fat dairy over red and processed meats.*

• **Incorporate High-Quality Plant Proteins:** *Include legumes, quinoa, and soy products regularly in your diet.*

Protein and Muscle Maintenance

Combatting Sarcopenia (Muscle Loss):

As we age, maintaining muscle becomes critical for mobility, strength, and overall health. Protein intake combined with regular resistance training can combat muscle loss.

Tips for Muscle Maintenance:

1. Consume High-Quality Protein: *Incorporate a mix of complete proteins, such as eggs, fish, or tofu.*

2. Leucine-Rich Foods: *Leucine, an amino acid found in eggs, dairy, and soy, is particularly effective for muscle protein synthesis.*

3. Strength Training: *Pair protein intake with regular weight-bearing exercises to preserve muscle mass.*

Examples of Balanced Protein-Rich Meals

1.**Breakfast:**

◦ *Overnight oats with almond butter, chia seeds, and a dollop of Greek yogurt.*

2.**Lunch:**

◦ *Quinoa salad with roasted chickpeas, avocado, and grilled chicken or tofu.*

3.**Dinner:**

◦ *Grilled salmon or tempeh with steamed vegetables and a side of farro.*

4.**Snacks:**

◦ *Hard-boiled eggs, a handful of nuts, or edamame.*

PLANT-BASED PROTEIN OPTIONS FOR LONGEVITY DIETS

For those aiming to reduce animal protein intake, here are high-protein plant-based options:

- **Soy Products:** *Tofu, tempeh, edamame (rich in complete protein).*

- **Lentils:** *18 grams of protein per cooked cup.*

- **Chickpeas:** *15 grams of protein per cooked cup.*

- **Quinoa:** *A complete protein with 8 grams per cooked cup.*

- **Nuts and Seeds:** *Almonds, peanuts, chia seeds, and hemp seeds provide a protein boost along with healthy fats.*

Cracking the Protein Puzzle

Protein is an essential piece of the longevity puzzle, but not all sources are created equal. A balanced approach that emphasizes plant-based proteins while incorporating lean animal proteins can support muscle maintenance, reduce inflammation, and lower the risk of chronic diseases.

By understanding your protein needs and diversifying your sources, you can create a sustainable dietary pattern that promotes vitality, strength, and longevity. Protein isn't just fuel for your muscles—it's a key ingredient in living a longer, healthier life.

CHAPTER 10
SUPERFOODS FOR SUPER AGING

Certain foods are nutritional powerhouses that offer exceptional benefits for health and longevity. These "superfoods" contain high levels of vitamins, minerals, antioxidants, and bioactive compounds that help combat inflammation, prevent chronic diseases, and slow the aging process. This chapter explores key superfoods to incorporate into your diet and the role of supplements in supporting optimal health.

Key Superfoods for Longevity

1. Berries: Nature's Antioxidant Powerhouses

Berries, such as blueberries, strawberries, raspberries, and blackberries, are rich in antioxidants, vitamins, and fiber.

Benefits of Berries:

• **Rich in Antioxidants:** *Combat free radicals and reduce oxidative stress, a major contributor to aging.*

• **Brain Health:** *Flavonoids in berries have been shown to improve memory and reduce cognitive decline.*

• **Heart Health:** *Lower blood pressure, improve cholesterol levels, and reduce the risk of cardiovascular diseases.*

How to Enjoy Berries:

• *Add to smoothies, oatmeal, or yogurt.*

• *Use as a topping for salads or desserts.*

• *Snack on them fresh or frozen.*

2. Leafy Greens: The Nutrient-Rich Staples

Leafy greens like spinach, kale, Swiss chard, and collard greens are loaded with vitamins, minerals, and phytochemicals.

Benefits of Leafy Greens:

• **Bone Health:** *High in vitamin K, which supports calcium absorption and bone strength.*

• **Eye Health:** *Contain lutein and zeaxanthin, which protect against age-related macular degeneration.*

• **Detoxification:** *Chlorophyll aids in cleansing the body and supporting liver health.*

How to Enjoy Leafy Greens:

• *Use as a base for salads.*

• *Blend into green smoothies or juices.*

• *Sauté with garlic and olive oil as a side dish.*

3. Turmeric: The Golden Healer

Turmeric, a bright yellow spice commonly used in Indian cuisine, contains curcumin, a compound with powerful anti-inflammatory and antioxidant properties.

Benefits of Turmeric:

• **Anti-Inflammatory Effects:** *Helps manage inflammation, a key driver of aging and chronic diseases.*

• **Brain Health:** *Curcumin may lower the risk of Alzheimer's disease by reducing amyloid plaque buildup.*

• **Joint Health:** *Eases symptoms of arthritis and supports joint mobility.*

How to Use Turmeric:

• *Add to curries, soups, and stews.*

• *Sprinkle on roasted vegetables or rice dishes.*

• *Drink as a turmeric latte or "golden milk."*

Pro Tip: Pair turmeric with black pepper to enhance curcumin absorption.

4. Green Tea: The Longevity Beverage

Green tea is packed with catechins, a type of antioxidant that promotes health and longevity. It has been consumed for centuries in cultures known for their long lifespans, such as Japan.

Benefits of Green Tea:

• **Heart Health:** *Lowers LDL cholesterol and improves blood vessel function.*

• **Weight Management:** *Boosts metabolism and aids in fat burning.*

• **Cancer Prevention:** *Catechins help prevent the growth of cancer cells.*

How to Enjoy Green Tea:

• *Drink freshly brewed green tea daily.*

• *Try matcha, a powdered form of green tea with even higher antioxidant levels.*

• *Add green tea to smoothies for a refreshing twist.*

Supplements: When and What to Consider

While a well-balanced diet should be your primary source of nutrients, supplements can be helpful in filling gaps, especially as we age and our nutritional needs change.

When to Consider Supplements

• **Nutrient Deficiencies:** *If blood tests reveal low levels of specific vitamins or minerals.*

• **Dietary Restrictions:** *If you follow a diet that excludes certain food groups, such as veganism.*

• **Age-Related Needs:** *Older adults may require more vitamin D, calcium, and B12.*

• **Chronic Conditions:** *Conditions like osteoporosis or anemia may necessitate targeted supplementation.*

Key Supplements for Longevity

1.**Vitamin D:**

◦ *Supports bone health, immune function, and mood regulation.*

◦ *Found in fatty fish, fortified foods, or synthesized through sunlight exposure.*

2.**Omega-3 Fatty Acids:**

◦ *Promote heart and brain health while reducing inflammation.*

◦ *Consider fish oil or algal oil supplements if dietary intake is insufficient.*

3.**Turmeric (Curcumin):**

◦ *For those who struggle to consume enough turmeric in their diet, curcumin capsules can provide a concentrated dose.*

4.**Probiotics:**

◦ *Improve gut health and support the immune system. Look for a supplement with diverse strains.*

5.Collagen:

◦ *Supports skin elasticity, joint health, and bone density.*

6.Magnesium:

◦ *Aids in muscle function, sleep quality, and heart health.*

How to Choose Quality Supplements

1.Check for Third-Party Testing:

◦ *Look for certifications from organizations like NSF, USP, or ConsumerLab to ensure purity and potency.*

2.Avoid Fillers and Additives:

◦ *Choose supplements with minimal ingredients and no artificial colors or sweeteners.*

3.Consult a Healthcare Professional:

◦ *Before starting any supplement, consult with a doctor or registered dietitian to ensure it's appropriate for your needs.*

Practical Tips for Incorporating Superfoods

1.Start Small:

◦ *Incorporate one new superfood into your diet each week to build lasting habits.*

2.Make It Enjoyable:

◦ *Experiment with recipes that make these foods delicious and accessible.*

3.Combine Superfoods:

◦ *For example, add berries, leafy greens, and green tea to a smoothie for a nutrient-packed meal.*

4.Stay Consistent:

○ *The benefits of superfoods come from regular consumption, not occasional indulgence.*

Nourishing Longevity With Superfoods

Superfoods are a simple yet powerful way to enhance your diet and support healthy aging. By incorporating nutrient-rich options like berries, leafy greens, turmeric, and green tea into your meals, you can fuel your body with the tools it needs to thrive.

Supplements can serve as a helpful complement, but they should never replace a balanced diet. Focus on whole, natural foods, and use supplements strategically to address specific needs. Remember, true health and longevity are built through consistent, mindful choices—and every bite counts.

CHAPTER 11
HYDRATION AND LONGEVITY

Water is the essence of life. It is essential for every biological process in the human body, from regulating temperature to removing waste. Despite its simplicity, proper hydration is often overlooked as a key factor in promoting longevity. This chapter explores the role of hydration in detoxification and cellular health, as well as the best drinks to support a long and vibrant life.

The Role of Hydration in Longevity

1. Water's Role in Detoxification

Hydration is critical for the body's detoxification systems, which work to remove waste and harmful substances.

- **Kidney Function:** *Water helps the kidneys filter toxins and waste products from the blood and excrete them in urine.*

- **Liver Support:** *Adequate hydration aids the liver in breaking down and eliminating toxins.*

- **Lymphatic System:** *Water keeps the lymph fluid circulating, which is vital for immune function and detoxification.*

2. Cellular Health and Longevity

Hydration is key to maintaining cellular health, which directly impacts aging and longevity.

• **Nutrient Transport:** *Water delivers essential nutrients to cells and removes waste products.*

• **Cell Membrane Integrity:** *Proper hydration supports cell membranes, helping cells maintain their function and structure.*

• **Energy Production:** *Water is involved in mitochondrial function, the powerhouse of cells, which produces energy for the body.*

• **Skin Health:** *Hydrated skin appears more youthful and resilient, reflecting overall cellular health.*

How Dehydration Accelerates Aging

Even mild dehydration can negatively impact the body, contributing to faster aging.

• **Cognitive Decline:** *Dehydration can impair brain function, leading to memory issues and fatigue.*

• **Joint Stiffness:** *Insufficient hydration reduces joint lubrication, causing stiffness and increasing the risk of injury.*

• **Toxin Accumulation:** *Chronic dehydration can lead to the buildup of toxins in the body, increasing inflammation and oxidative stress.*

• **Skin Aging:** *Dehydrated skin is more prone to wrinkles and fine lines due to loss of elasticity.*

The Best Drinks for a Long Life

1. Water: The Ultimate Hydration Source

• **Benefits:** *Zero calories, widely available, and essential for all bodily functions.*

- **Pro Tip:** *Aim for at least 8–10 cups (2–2.5 liters) of water daily, but adjust based on activity level, climate, and age.*

2. *Herbal Teas*

Herbal teas like chamomile, peppermint, and rooibos offer hydration along with additional health benefits.

- **Chamomile:** *Promotes relaxation and better sleep.*

- **Peppermint:** *Aids digestion and reduces inflammation.*

- **Rooibos:** *Packed with antioxidants that support heart health.*

3. *Green Tea*

As mentioned in Chapter 10, green tea is a longevity beverage rich in catechins that reduce inflammation, support brain health, and promote heart health.

4. *Infused Water*

Adding fruits, herbs, or vegetables to water enhances flavor and provides a nutrient boost.

- **Examples:** *Lemon and cucumber water, mint and berry water, or ginger and orange water.*

5. *Coconut Water*

- **Benefits:** *A natural source of electrolytes, coconut water helps replenish lost fluids after exercise or on hot days.*

- **Caution:** *Choose unsweetened varieties to avoid excess sugar.*

6. *Bone Broth*

- **Benefits:** *Packed with collagen, amino acids, and minerals, bone broth supports joint health, skin elasticity, and gut health.*

7. *Freshly Pressed Vegetable Juices*

• **Benefits:** *Concentrated sources of vitamins and minerals, particularly when made with greens like kale, spinach, and celery.*

• **Pro Tip:** *Limit fruit content to avoid excessive sugar.*

Hydration Tips for Longevity

1.**Start Your Day with Water:**

◦ *Drink a glass of water first thing in the morning to rehydrate after sleep.*

2.**Carry a Reusable Water Bottle:**

◦ *Keep water accessible throughout the day to encourage regular sipping.*

3.**Set Hydration Goals:**

◦ *Use apps or reminders to track water intake and stay consistent.*

4.**Eat Water-Rich Foods:**

◦ *Incorporate foods with high water content, such as watermelon, cucumbers, oranges, and celery.*

5.**Monitor Hydration Status:**

◦ *Check the color of your urine—it should be pale yellow.*

When and How Much to Drink

Timing Matters:

• **Morning:** *Start your day with a glass of water.*

• **Pre-Meal:** *Drinking water before meals can aid digestion and prevent overeating.*

• **Exercise:** *Stay hydrated before, during, and after physical activity.*

• **Evening:** *Avoid excessive hydration right before bed to prevent interrupted sleep.*

Individual Needs:

Hydration needs vary based on factors such as:

- *Body size and composition.*

- *Activity levels.*

- *Climate and temperature.*

- *Health conditions (e.g., kidney or heart disease).*

What to Avoid

Certain drinks can have negative effects on hydration and overall health.

- **Sugary Beverages:** *Sodas, energy drinks, and sweetened juices contribute empty calories and can increase the risk of chronic diseases.*

- **Excessive Caffeine:** *While moderate coffee and tea consumption have health benefits, excessive caffeine can lead to dehydration and disrupted sleep.*

- **Alcohol:** *Alcohol acts as a diuretic, leading to fluid loss and potential dehydration.*

Hydration and Longevity: A Case Study

Studies of populations in Blue Zones—regions with the longest-lived individuals—highlight the importance of hydration habits. For example:

- *In Okinawa, Japan, people drink plenty of herbal teas, including jasmine tea, which is rich in antioxidants.*

- *In Ikaria, Greece, herbal infusions made from sage, rosemary, and wild oregano are staples that promote hydration and reduce inflammation.*

Drink to Your Health

Hydration is a simple yet powerful tool for promoting longevity and vitality. Water plays a crucial role in detoxification, cellular health, and preventing the effects of aging. By choosing the right beverages—such as water, green tea, herbal teas, and nutrient-rich infusions—you can support your body's natural processes and enhance your overall quality of life.

Remember, staying hydrated is not just about drinking enough water but also about making mindful choices that align with your health goals. Small, consistent habits can make a big difference in your journey to a longer, healthier life.

CHAPTER 12
THE TIMING OF EATING

When it comes to longevity and healthy aging, the timing of your meals may be just as important as what you eat. Research into intermittent fasting and time-restricted eating has shown that the hours during which you consume food can play a significant role in cellular repair, metabolism, and longevity. This chapter explores how the timing of eating impacts aging and how adjusting your eating habits can enhance your healthspan.

The Science of Eating Timing

The body's natural processes, including digestion, metabolism, and cell repair, follow a circadian rhythm. This internal clock regulates various bodily functions, including when we are most efficient at digesting and absorbing nutrients. By aligning your eating habits with these rhythms, you can improve your body's ability to process food and enhance its regenerative functions.

Intermittent Fasting and Time-Restricted Eating

1. Intermittent Fasting (IF): A Powerful Longevity Tool

Intermittent fasting is an eating pattern that alternates between periods of eating and fasting. It doesn't specify what foods to eat but focuses on when to eat, limiting the time window in which food is consumed.

Key Types of Intermittent Fasting:

• **16/8 Method:** *This is one of the most popular methods, where you fast for 16 hours and eat within an 8-hour window.*

• **5:2 Method:** *You eat normally for five days of the week and restrict calorie intake to about 500–600 calories on the other two days.*

• **Alternate Day Fasting:** *You alternate between fasting and eating normally every other day.*

Benefits of Intermittent Fasting for Longevity:

• **Cellular Repair and Autophagy:** *Fasting triggers a process called autophagy, where the body cleans out damaged cells and regenerates new, healthy ones. This is linked to reduced aging and improved health.*

• **Improved Metabolic Health:** *IF can help regulate blood sugar levels, improve insulin sensitivity, and reduce the risk of type 2 diabetes.*

• **Reduced Inflammation:** *IF has been shown to reduce markers of inflammation, a key factor in aging and the development of chronic diseases.*

• **Increased Longevity:** *Animal studies have shown that intermittent fasting can extend lifespan by improving mitochondrial function and reducing oxidative stress.*

2. Time-Restricted Eating (TRE): Eating Within a Defined Window

Time-restricted eating is a form of intermittent fasting where you limit the daily eating window to a specific period, such as 8–10 hours, and fast for the remaining 14–16 hours. For example, you may eat between 8:00 AM and 4:00 PM and fast from 4:00 PM to 8:00 AM the next day.

How TRE Works:

• The idea is to consume all meals during a set window of time, allowing your body to enter a fasting state for the rest of the day. This fasting period supports metabolic processes and optimizes cellular repair.

Benefits of Time-Restricted Eating:

• Improved Circadian Rhythms: *TRE aligns food consumption with your body's natural circadian rhythm, leading to more efficient digestion and energy regulation.*

• Weight Management: *TRE may help reduce overeating and late-night snacking, promoting weight loss and improving body composition.*

• Brain Health: *Studies show that TRE can improve cognitive function and may lower the risk of neurodegenerative diseases like Alzheimer's.*

• Reduced Risk of Chronic Diseases: *Time-restricted eating may lower the risk of heart disease, diabetes, and certain cancers by improving metabolic health and reducing oxidative stress.*

How Meal Timing Impacts Aging

1. The Role of Insulin and Metabolism

Insulin, a hormone that regulates blood sugar, plays a central role in aging. When we eat, insulin levels spike to help absorb nutrients from food into the cells. Chronic high insulin levels, often resulting from overeating or eating frequently, contribute to insulin resistance and accelerated aging.

Meal Timing and Insulin Sensitivity:

• Fasting: *Periods of fasting allow insulin levels to drop, giving the body time to repair itself and reduce insulin resistance.*

• Frequent Meals: *Eating frequently throughout the day can lead to persistent elevated insulin levels, which can promote inflammation and increase the risk of chronic diseases like heart disease and diabetes.*

2. Hormonal Health and Longevity

Meal timing can also influence key hormones involved in aging, including growth hormone and cortisol.

• **Growth Hormone:** *This hormone is essential for muscle repair, fat metabolism, and tissue growth. Fasting increases the production of growth hormone, which helps prevent the muscle loss and metabolic decline that often occur with aging.*

• **Cortisol:** *Eating late at night can interfere with the production of cortisol, the stress hormone, leading to poor sleep quality and higher levels of chronic stress.*

3. Digestive Rest and Longevity

Your digestive system needs time to rest and recover. Eating constantly throughout the day doesn't allow your digestive system adequate recovery time. By fasting or eating within a restricted window, you give your digestive system a chance to rest, leading to more efficient nutrient absorption and better overall health.

Practical Tips for Implementing Time-Restricted Eating

1.Start Gradually:

◦ *If you're new to intermittent fasting, start by shortening your eating window gradually. Begin by eating within a 12-hour window and work your way down to 8–10 hours.*

2.Listen to Your Body:

◦ *Pay attention to hunger cues and avoid forcing yourself to eat when you're not hungry. Fasting should feel natural, not stressful.*

3.Stay Hydrated:

◦ *Drink plenty of water, herbal teas, or black coffee during fasting periods to stay hydrated and curb hunger.*

4.Choose Nutrient-Dense Meals:

◦ *Make the most of your eating window by focusing on whole, nutrient-dense foods. Prioritize vegetables, lean proteins, healthy fats, and complex carbohydrates.*

5.Avoid Late-Night Eating:

◦ *Try to finish your last meal of the day at least 2–3 hours before bedtime. Late-night eating can disrupt sleep and interfere with the body's natural repair processes.*

Common Concerns About Intermittent Fasting

1. Will I Feel Hungry or Irritable?

• *Many people experience hunger during the initial phase of intermittent fasting, but it usually diminishes as the body adapts to the new eating schedule. Drinking plenty of water and eating nutrient-rich meals during the eating window can help manage hunger.*

2. Can I Exercise While Fasting?

• *Exercise can be safely performed during fasting periods, especially light to moderate activities like walking, yoga, or strength training. If you plan to do high-intensity exercise, consider adjusting your eating window to ensure adequate fuel.*

3. Is Intermittent Fasting Safe for Everyone?

• *While intermittent fasting is generally safe for most people, it may not be appropriate for those with certain health conditions, such as diabetes, or for pregnant or breastfeeding women. Always consult a healthcare professional before starting a fasting regimen.*

Harnessing the Power of Meal Timing for Longevity

The timing of your meals can have a profound impact on your aging process. Intermittent fasting and time-restricted eating offer powerful benefits for metabolism, cellular repair, and overall health. By aligning your eating habits with your body's natural rhythms, you can reduce inflammation, improve hormone balance, and promote longevity.

Adopting a fasting regimen may take time, but the long-term benefits for your healthspan and lifespan are worth the effort. By choosing when to eat wisely, you are giving your body the tools it needs to thrive well into old age.

CHAPTER 13
THE ROLE OF PHYSICAL ACTIVITY

Physical activity is one of the most powerful tools in promoting longevity. It not only enhances cardiovascular and muscular health but also influences mental well-being and the body's ability to repair itself. While structured exercise—such as weight training, cardio, and stretching—is essential for maintaining physical function, the role of everyday movement cannot be underestimated. This chapter explores the benefits of physical activity for longevity, focusing on building strength, endurance, and flexibility, as well as the importance of non-exercise activity in maintaining overall health.

Building Strength, Endurance, and Flexibility

1. Strength Training: The Foundation of Longevity

As we age, we naturally lose muscle mass, a condition known as sarcopenia. This loss of muscle not only affects strength and mobility but also contributes to higher risks of falls, fractures, and metabolic diseases. Building and maintaining muscle mass through strength training is critical for overall longevity.

Benefits of Strength Training:

• **Improved Metabolism:** *Muscle tissue burns more calories at rest than fat tissue, helping to maintain a healthy weight and prevent metabolic diseases like type 2 diabetes.*

• **Bone Health:** *Resistance training strengthens bones and reduces the risk of osteoporosis and fractures.*

• **Joint Health:** *Strengthening muscles around the joints helps improve stability, reduce pain, and prevent injuries.*

• **Cognitive Benefits:** *Recent research shows that strength training can enhance brain health, improve memory, and reduce the risk of neurodegenerative diseases.*

How to Incorporate Strength Training:

• **Bodyweight Exercises:** *Push-ups, squats, lunges, and planks are excellent bodyweight exercises that require no equipment.*

• **Free Weights or Machines:** *Dumbbells, kettlebells, or resistance machines can help target specific muscle groups.*

• **Progressive Overload:** *Gradually increase the intensity or weight in your strength training routine to continue building muscle and strength.*

2. Endurance: Cardiovascular Health and Stamina

Cardiovascular activity is essential for heart health and overall vitality. Regular endurance exercise strengthens the heart, improves circulation, and supports lung capacity, all of which are critical for healthy aging.

Benefits of Endurance Training:

• **Heart Health:** *Regular aerobic exercise improves heart function, reduces high blood pressure, and decreases the risk of heart disease and stroke.*

• **Enhanced Circulation:** *Cardiovascular activity improves blood flow, allowing oxygen and nutrients to reach muscles and organs more efficiently.*

- **Weight Management:** *Cardio burns calories and helps maintain a healthy weight, reducing the risk of obesity-related diseases like diabetes and hypertension.*

- **Mental Health:** *Aerobic exercise releases endorphins, which improve mood, reduce stress, and fight anxiety and depression.*

How to Incorporate Endurance Training:

- **Walking and Hiking:** *One of the easiest ways to improve endurance is simply by walking. Aim for brisk walks of 30–45 minutes most days of the week.*

- **Cycling or Swimming:** *Low-impact activities like cycling and swimming provide excellent cardiovascular benefits without putting undue strain on the joints.*

- **Dancing or Jogging:** *Both are great forms of endurance exercise that combine fun with fitness.*

3. Flexibility: Maintaining Range of Motion

Flexibility is key for mobility, reducing injury risk, and maintaining independence as we age. Regular stretching and flexibility exercises help keep muscles and joints supple, preventing stiffness and discomfort.

Benefits of Flexibility Training:

- **Joint Health:** *Regular stretching helps lubricate the joints, reducing the risk of arthritis and improving flexibility.*

- **Posture and Alignment:** *Flexibility exercises enhance posture, which is important for overall alignment and preventing back and neck pain.*

- **Balance and Coordination:** *Stretching improves coordination and balance, reducing the risk of falls.*

- **Injury Prevention:** *A flexible body is less prone to strains, sprains, and overuse injuries.*

How to Incorporate Flexibility Training:

• **Yoga:** *Yoga is a powerful practice that promotes flexibility, strength, and relaxation.*

• **Pilates:** *Pilates focuses on stretching and strengthening the core and back muscles.*

• **Dynamic and Static Stretching:** *Incorporate both dynamic stretches (e.g., leg swings, arm circles) before exercise and static stretches (e.g., hamstring stretch, quad stretch) after exercise to maintain flexibility.*

The Importance of Non-Exercise Activity

While formal exercise is essential, non-exercise activity—those small movements we engage in throughout the day—also plays a crucial role in promoting longevity. People in Blue Zones, regions where individuals live the longest and healthiest lives, tend to be highly active in daily life without necessarily engaging in structured workouts.

1. Daily Movement vs. Structured Exercise

Non-exercise activity thermogenesis (NEAT) refers to the calories burned through everyday activities, such as walking, gardening, cleaning, or standing. Although NEAT doesn't involve formal exercise, it can have a significant impact on overall health and longevity.

Examples of Non-Exercise Activity:

• **Walking or Cycling to Work:** *Instead of sitting in a car or bus, consider walking or biking to your destination whenever possible.*

• **Gardening or Yard Work:** *Gardening is a great way to burn calories while enjoying the outdoors.*

• **Housework:** *Activities like vacuuming, dusting, or doing laundry count as movement and can keep you active.*

- **Standing More Often:** *Standing instead of sitting throughout the day can make a big difference in metabolic health.*

2. Reducing Sedentary Behavior

One of the biggest threats to longevity in modern society is prolonged sitting. Sitting for long periods has been associated with increased risk of heart disease, type 2 diabetes, and early death. Even if you exercise regularly, sitting for extended periods can negate some of the benefits of exercise.

Strategies to Reduce Sedentary Time:

- **Take Breaks:** *Stand up, stretch, or walk around for a few minutes every hour.*

- **Use a Standing Desk:** *Consider using a standing desk or a convertible desk that allows you to alternate between sitting and standing.*

- **Use Pedometers or Fitness Trackers:** *Wearable devices can help remind you to move and track your steps throughout the day.*

Practical Tips for Incorporating Physical Activity into Daily Life

1.Find Activities You Enjoy:

◦ *Whether it's dancing, swimming, or playing tennis, doing activities you love makes it easier to stay consistent.*

2.Incorporate Movement into Routine Tasks:

◦ *Take the stairs instead of the elevator, walk or bike to nearby errands, or take a walk after dinner.*

3.Set Goals and Track Progress:

◦ *Set realistic fitness goals—whether it's a step count, weight-lifting target, or stretching routine—and track your progress to stay motivated.*

4.Get Outside:

◦ *Spending time outdoors in nature has numerous health benefits, including stress reduction, improved mood, and enhanced physical activity.*

5.Make Physical Activity Social:

◦ *Join a walking group, take a yoga class with a friend, or join a recreational sports team. Social engagement enhances motivation and consistency.*

Move for a Longer, Healthier Life

Physical activity is a cornerstone of longevity. Whether it's through strength training, cardiovascular exercise, flexibility work, or simply moving more throughout the day, staying active promotes health at every age. Non-exercise activity, often overlooked, is just as important for maintaining metabolic health, muscle mass, and a positive mindset.

By making movement a regular part of your daily routine, you'll improve your quality of life, prevent disease, and increase your chances of aging gracefully. Whether through formal exercise or simple daily tasks, staying active is one of the most reliable ways to support a long, healthy life.

CHAPTER 14
SLEEP: THE ULTIMATE RESET

Sleep is often underestimated when it comes to longevity. However, it is one of the most crucial factors for a long, healthy life. Sleep not only allows your body and mind to rest but also serves as a time for rejuvenation, healing, and cellular repair. In this chapter, we will explore how sleep influences longevity and offer practical strategies for building the perfect sleep routine to enhance health and well-being.

How Sleep Rejuvenates the Body and Mind

1. Cellular Repair and Regeneration

During sleep, the body is in a state of repair and restoration. Growth hormone, which is essential for muscle and tissue repair, is released during deep sleep stages. This process supports cellular repair, strengthens the immune system, and helps maintain healthy tissues. Without enough sleep, this critical repair process is compromised, leading to a greater risk of disease and aging.

Key Processes That Happen During Sleep:

• **Cellular Repair:** *Cells regenerate, replace damaged tissues, and perform other restorative functions.*

• **Immune Function:** *Sleep strengthens the immune system, helping the body defend itself against infections and diseases.*

• **Muscle Repair:** *Deep sleep enhances muscle recovery after physical activity, preventing muscle loss and promoting strength.*

• **Hormonal Balance:** *Sleep helps regulate hormones, including cortisol (stress hormone) and insulin (which controls blood sugar).*

2. Cognitive Function and Brain Health

Sleep is essential for brain health, and chronic sleep deprivation has been linked to cognitive decline, memory loss, and an increased risk of neurological diseases like Alzheimer's. During sleep, the brain consolidates memories, processes information, and clears waste products.

Brain Benefits of Sleep:

• **Memory Consolidation:** *Sleep helps the brain solidify new memories, improving learning and recall.*

• **Mental Clarity:** *Adequate sleep improves focus, decision-making, and cognitive performance.*

• **Detoxification:** *During sleep, the brain activates the glymphatic system, which clears waste products like beta-amyloid that contribute to neurodegenerative diseases.*

• **Emotional Regulation:** *Sleep regulates mood and helps manage stress, anxiety, and depression, improving emotional resilience.*

3. Metabolic Health and Weight Management

Sleep plays a key role in regulating appetite and metabolism. Poor sleep disrupts the balance of hunger hormones like leptin and ghrelin, which control satiety and hunger. Sleep deprivation increases cravings for unhealthy foods, especially those high in sugar and fat, which can lead to weight gain and metabolic dysfunction.

Sleep's Impact on Metabolism:

• **Improved Insulin Sensitivity:** *Adequate sleep enhances insulin sensitivity, reducing the risk of type 2 diabetes and obesity.*

• **Hunger Regulation:** *A lack of sleep leads to increased hunger and cravings, making it harder to maintain a healthy weight.*

• **Increased Fat Storage:** *Sleep deprivation is associated with increased fat storage, particularly abdominal fat.*

4. Stress Reduction and Emotional Health

Sleep is a powerful stress reliever. When we sleep, cortisol levels drop, allowing the body to relax and recover from the day's stress. Chronic sleep deprivation, on the other hand, increases cortisol levels, leading to chronic stress, anxiety, and an increased risk of heart disease.

The Connection Between Sleep and Stress:

• **Stress Reduction:** *Deep sleep promotes relaxation, reduces cortisol, and helps manage emotional stress.*

• **Mental Resilience:** *Well-rested individuals are better equipped to handle stress and emotional challenges.*

• **Mood Improvement:** *Sleep stabilizes mood, enhancing emotional well-being and reducing symptoms of anxiety and depression.*

Building the Perfect Sleep Routine

Creating a consistent and restorative sleep routine is key to ensuring that your body and mind reap the full benefits of sleep. A well-established routine helps signal to your body that it's time to wind down, improving both the quality and duration of your sleep.

1. Create a Sleep-Friendly Environment

The environment in which you sleep can significantly impact sleep quality. Here are a few strategies to make your bedroom conducive to restful sleep:

• **Keep it Cool:** *The optimal sleep temperature is around 65°F (18°C). A cooler room promotes deeper sleep.*

• **Limit Light Exposure:** *Exposure to bright light before bed can interfere with melatonin production, the hormone responsible for regulating sleep. Use blackout curtains or sleep masks to block out light, and avoid screens (phones, tablets, computers) for at least an hour before bed.*

• **Reduce Noise:** *Minimize noise in your sleep environment, or use white noise or calming sounds to help you fall asleep.*

• **Invest in Comfort:** *A comfortable mattress and pillows tailored to your sleep position are essential for quality rest.*

2. Establish a Consistent Sleep Schedule

Going to bed and waking up at the same time each day helps regulate your internal clock and improves sleep quality. Try to maintain a consistent sleep schedule, even on weekends, to keep your circadian rhythm in sync.

Tips for Consistency:

• **Set a Bedtime:** *Choose a bedtime that allows for at least 7–9 hours of sleep each night.*

• **Wake Up at the Same Time:** *Even if you've had a poor night's sleep, waking up at the same time each day helps train your body to follow a regular sleep-wake pattern.*

• **Limit Naps:** *If you nap during the day, limit it to 20–30 minutes, and avoid napping too late in the afternoon.*

3. Relax Before Bed

Incorporating a wind-down routine can help signal to your body that it's time to sleep. Avoid engaging in stimulating activities like work, intense exercise, or watching exciting TV shows right before bed. Instead, engage in calming activities that help lower stress and prepare the body for sleep.

Relaxing Pre-Sleep Activities:

• **Reading a Book:** *Choose light reading material that doesn't overstimulate your mind.*

• **Gentle Yoga or Stretching:** *Gentle stretches or yoga poses can relax the body and release tension.*

• **Deep Breathing or Meditation:** *Mindfulness techniques, like deep breathing or meditation, can calm the nervous system and promote relaxation.*

• **Journaling:** *Writing down your thoughts can help clear your mind, reducing anxiety or stress.*

4. Avoid Stimulants and Heavy Meals

Certain substances and activities can disrupt sleep quality, especially if consumed too close to bedtime.

What to Avoid Before Bed:

• **Caffeine:** *Caffeine, found in coffee, tea, and some sodas, can stay in the body for hours and interfere with sleep. Avoid caffeine for at least 6 hours before bed.*

• **Alcohol:** *While alcohol can make you feel drowsy initially, it disrupts the deeper stages of sleep and can cause frequent awakenings during the night.*

• **Heavy Meals:** *Large or spicy meals can cause indigestion, which may disturb sleep. Avoid eating large meals within 2–3 hours of bedtime.*

• **Excessive Fluids:** *Drinking too much liquid before bed can lead to frequent trips to the bathroom during the night, disrupting sleep.*

Sleep Supplements: What Works?

While a healthy sleep routine is the most effective way to improve sleep, certain supplements may help support the process. Before using supplements, it's important to address underlying factors that may be affecting your sleep, such as stress or poor habits.

Common Sleep Supplements:

• **Melatonin:** *Melatonin is a hormone that regulates sleep-wake cycles. It may be helpful for people who have irregular sleep schedules or difficulty falling asleep.*

• **Magnesium:** *This mineral plays a role in muscle relaxation and sleep regulation. Magnesium supplementation may promote relaxation and reduce symptoms of insomnia.*

• **Valerian Root:** *An herb that has been traditionally used as a sleep aid. Some studies suggest it may help improve sleep quality.*

• **Lavender:** *Aromatherapy with lavender essential oil has been shown to promote relaxation and improve sleep quality.*

Sleep Your Way to Longevity

Sleep is the ultimate reset button for the body and mind, supporting everything from immune function and cellular repair to brain health and emotional resilience. By building a consistent and restorative sleep routine, you can optimize your health and improve your chances of living a long, vibrant life.

Prioritize sleep by creating a peaceful environment, sticking to a consistent schedule, and engaging in relaxation practices before bed. With good sleep, your body has the opportunity to heal, regenerate, and rejuvenate, ensuring that you wake up ready to face each day with energy and vitality.

CHAPTER 15
CONNECTION AND COMMUNITY

Humans are inherently social beings, and one of the most powerful influences on longevity is the quality of our relationships. Connection with others not only provides emotional support but also directly impacts our physical and mental health. In this chapter, we will explore the science behind relationships and their role in longevity, as well as practical strategies for building supportive social circles that promote health and well-being.

The Science of Relationships and Longevity

1. The Impact of Strong Relationships on Health

Research has shown that strong, supportive relationships can significantly improve lifespan. Studies in Blue Zones—regions where people live longer than average—demonstrate that community and connection play key roles in promoting healthy aging. The social bonds we form have a direct effect on our health, influencing everything from stress levels to immune function.

How Relationships Influence Longevity:

• **Lower Stress Levels:** *Strong social support helps buffer the effects of stress. When we feel supported, we experience lower levels of cortisol (the* *stress hormone), which helps reduce the negative impacts of stress on the body.*

• **Reduced Risk of Depression and Anxiety:** *Social connections provide emotional support, reduce feelings of loneliness, and can help ward off mental health challenges such as depression and anxiety.*

• **Improved Immune Function:** *Positive relationships can boost the immune system, helping the body fight off infections and reduce the risk of chronic diseases.*

• **Better Heart Health:** *Having a strong support network has been linked to lower blood pressure, reduced risk of cardiovascular disease, and improved recovery from illness or surgery.*

• **Increased Life Satisfaction:** *Relationships provide a sense of purpose, fulfillment, and happiness, contributing to overall well-being and longevity.*

2. The Role of Social Connections in Aging Well

As we age, social connections become even more important. Older adults with strong social networks tend to live longer, healthier lives. Isolation and loneliness, on the other hand, have been linked to numerous negative health outcomes, including an increased risk of mortality.

The Longevity Benefits of Connection:

• **Longevity in Blue Zones:** *In regions like Okinawa, Japan, and Sardinia, Italy, social connectedness is a key part of daily life. People in these areas often live well into their 90s or beyond, surrounded by close-knit families and communities.*

• **Intergenerational Connections:** *Older adults who maintain relationships with younger generations often experience higher levels of vitality and purpose. These intergenerational bonds provide a sense of belonging and contribute to better mental health.*

- **Community Involvement:** *Being part of a community or group can provide a sense of purpose and prevent feelings of isolation, both of which are critical for long-term well-being.*

Building Supportive Social Circles

1. Nurturing Meaningful Relationships

While having a large number of acquaintances can be beneficial, the depth and quality of our relationships have the most impact on longevity. Meaningful relationships are those in which we feel loved, understood, and supported. These deep connections are vital for maintaining mental and emotional health as we age.

Strategies for Building Strong, Supportive Relationships:

- **Prioritize Quality Over Quantity:** *Focus on cultivating a few close, supportive relationships rather than trying to maintain a large circle of acquaintances.*

- **Be Present:** *Building strong relationships requires time and attention. Be present with loved ones, listen actively, and offer emotional support when needed.*

- **Communicate Openly:** *Honest communication fosters trust and deepens connections. Be open about your needs and emotions, and encourage others to do the same.*

- **Practice Empathy:** *Understanding and empathizing with others helps strengthen bonds and fosters a sense of mutual care.*

2. Engage in Group Activities

Being part of a group—whether it's a social club, exercise class, volunteer group, or religious community—provides both social interaction and a sense of belonging. Participating in group activities increases opportunities for bonding, reduces isolation, and enhances overall life satisfaction.

Benefits of Group Engagement:

• **Social Interaction:** *Regular interaction with others helps improve cognitive function, reduces the risk of depression, and fosters a sense of community.*

• **Shared Experiences:** *Engaging in group activities creates opportunities for shared experiences, which can strengthen emotional connections and increase life satisfaction.*

• **Physical and Mental Health Benefits:** *Participating in group exercise or activities can improve physical health, mental well-being, and motivation.*

3. Strengthening Family Ties

Family often plays a central role in longevity. Whether biological or chosen, family members provide emotional support, care during illness, and a sense of stability and belonging. In Blue Zones, families are often the cornerstone of a person's social network, and maintaining close relationships with family members is one of the key factors in aging well.

How to Strengthen Family Ties:

• **Create Traditions:** *Establishing family traditions—whether it's weekly dinners, vacations, or celebrations—helps maintain strong family bonds and creates lasting memories.*

• **Spend Quality Time Together:** *Set aside time to engage in meaningful activities with family, whether it's enjoying a meal together, taking walks, or sharing stories.*

• **Supportive Roles:** *Offer and accept help from family members, particularly as you age. Being a caregiver or receiving care strengthens the emotional bond and builds resilience.*

4. Finding Community Through Shared Interests

Sometimes, creating a social circle requires seeking out groups or communities that share your passions and interests. Whether it's a hobby, sport, or charitable cause, finding like-minded people can help you feel connected and supported.

Ways to Find Like-Minded Communities:

• **Join a Club or Class:** *Take a class or join a club that aligns with your interests, whether it's art, dance, literature, or fitness.*

• **Volunteer:** *Volunteering not only benefits others but also provides opportunities to meet new people and create meaningful connections.*

• **Online Communities:** *If physical proximity is a challenge, online communities focused on shared interests or hobbies can provide emotional support and a sense of belonging.*

THE ROLE OF SPIRITUALITY AND FAITH

For many people, spirituality and faith play a key role in fostering social connection and providing purpose. Whether through formal religious practices or personal spiritual beliefs, having a sense of connection to something larger than oneself can increase resilience and promote mental and emotional well-being.

Spirituality and Longevity:

• **Sense of Purpose:** *Spiritual beliefs often provide a deep sense of purpose and meaning in life, which contributes to greater life satisfaction and longevity.*

• **Community Support:** *Many religious or spiritual groups offer a strong sense of community and support, which can help individuals navigate difficult times and enhance emotional well-being.*

• **Resilience in Facing Life's Challenges:** *Spirituality can provide individuals with coping strategies and emotional strength during challenging times, contributing to improved mental health and longevity.*

The Power of Connection

Connection and community are essential for a long, healthy life. Building and maintaining strong relationships—whether with family, friends, or community members—has a profound impact on both physical and mental health. Humans are wired for connection, and nurturing those bonds not only provides emotional support but also contributes to longevity.

By prioritizing meaningful relationships, engaging in community activities, and staying connected to loved ones, you can boost your chances of living a longer, more fulfilling life. Remember, it's not just the number of people in your life that matters, but the depth and quality of your relationships that make all the difference.

CHAPTER 16
HOBBIES AND LIFELONG LEARNING

One of the most important aspects of living a long and fulfilling life is keeping the brain engaged and active throughout the years. Lifelong learning and pursuing hobbies that stimulate the mind and body are key ingredients in the longevity blueprint. In this chapter, we will explore how keeping the brain active with new skills, passions, and intellectual curiosity plays a pivotal role in healthy aging and overall well-being.

Keeping the Brain Active with New Skills and Passions

1. The Importance of Cognitive Engagement

As we age, the brain undergoes natural changes. However, studies show that intellectual engagement—such as learning new skills, hobbies, or languages—can help maintain brain health and even slow cognitive decline. Activities that challenge the brain create new neural pathways, enhancing cognitive flexibility and resilience against conditions like dementia and Alzheimer's disease.

How New Skills Benefit the Brain:

- **Neuroplasticity:** *The brain has the ability to reorganize itself by* *forming new neural connections. Engaging in activities that stimulate the mind can strengthen these connections and improve brain function.*

• **Memory Enhancement:** *Learning new skills or information improves memory recall and keeps the brain sharp.*

• **Problem-Solving and Critical Thinking:** *Challenging the brain with puzzles, new activities, or learning opportunities helps improve problem-solving abilities and cognitive flexibility.*

• **Reduced Risk of Cognitive Decline:** *Studies show that those who engage in lifelong learning are less likely to experience cognitive decline and neurodegenerative diseases as they age.*

2. Hobbies as a Tool for Cognitive Health

Hobbies that require both mental and physical engagement—such as playing an instrument, learning a new language, painting, or solving puzzles—are especially effective in keeping the brain agile. These hobbies also provide a sense of accomplishment, joy, and fulfillment, which contributes to emotional well-being.

Examples of Brain-Boosting Hobbies:

• **Music:** *Learning an instrument or singing can stimulate multiple areas of the brain, improving memory, coordination, and emotional expression.*

• **Art and Craft:** *Creative pursuits like painting, drawing, or sculpting not only promote cognitive engagement but also allow for self-expression, boosting mental health.*

• **Language Learning:** *Acquiring a new language enhances cognitive function, improves memory, and fosters cultural appreciation.*

• **Chess or Strategy Games:** *Games that involve strategy, planning, and critical thinking can improve decision-making and memory.*

• **Writing or Journaling:** *Writing, whether for pleasure or personal reflection, is a creative and cognitive exercise that helps enhance communication and memory.*

The Importance of Curiosity

1. A Curious Mind Keeps You Young

Curiosity is one of the most powerful tools for lifelong learning. It keeps the mind active and engaged, encouraging exploration and the pursuit of new knowledge. People who remain curious throughout their lives tend to have a more positive outlook, higher levels of creativity, and greater resilience in the face of challenges.

How Curiosity Impacts Longevity:

• **Mental Agility:** *Curious people are constantly seeking new information and experiences, which keeps their brains agile and adaptive.*

• **Increased Life Satisfaction:** *Engaging with new topics or activities satisfies the innate human desire for learning, leading to greater happiness and fulfillment.*

• **Stress Reduction:** *Curiosity can help take the focus off negative emotions or stress, shifting attention toward exploration and discovery.*

• **Sense of Purpose:** *A curious mindset fosters a sense of purpose by encouraging personal growth, skill development, and new accomplishments.*

2. Staying Open to New Experiences

Curiosity leads to the exploration of new experiences—whether it's trying a new sport, visiting a new place, or learning a new craft. These new experiences stimulate the brain, promote adaptability, and increase social interaction, all of which are essential for longevity.

Ways to Cultivate Curiosity:

• **Try New Things:** *Commit to exploring something new every month, whether it's a new hobby, a new place, or a new idea.*

• **Ask Questions:** *Stay curious by asking questions, seeking out new information, and diving deeper into topics that interest you.*

• **Be Open to Change:** *Cultivate an open mindset that allows you to embrace new opportunities, whether in your career, social life, or personal development.*

• **Travel and Explore:** *Traveling, even locally, exposes you to new cultures, perspectives, and experiences, all of which can foster personal growth and stimulate curiosity.*

Lifelong Learning and the Social Benefits

1. Learning Together Builds Stronger Connections

Learning doesn't have to be a solitary pursuit. Engaging in group activities, attending classes, or joining social groups that share your interests can enhance both cognitive and social well-being. Social learning fosters connection, which plays a vital role in mental and emotional health, as we saw in Chapter 15 on relationships and community.

Social Learning Opportunities:

• **Workshops and Classes:** *Enroll in community-based workshops or courses where you can learn new skills alongside others, creating an opportunity for social interaction.*

• **Clubs and Interest Groups:** *Join clubs related to hobbies such as book clubs, gardening groups, or cooking classes. These groups offer both social connection and intellectual stimulation.*

• **Online Learning Communities:** *Platforms like Coursera, Master-Class , etc.*

CHAPTER 17
NATURE'S HEALING POWER

In today's fast-paced, technology-driven world, it's easy to forget the profound impact that nature has on our physical, mental, and emotional well-being. Time spent outdoors has been linked to a host of health benefits, including improved stress management, enhanced mood, and even greater longevity. In this chapter, we will explore the healing power of nature and how spending time outdoors, soaking up sunlight, and breathing fresh air can significantly improve our health and contribute to a longer, healthier life.

Time Outdoors and Its Effects on Stress and Health

1. The Stress-Reducing Effects of Nature

Stress is one of the most significant factors contributing to poor health and premature aging. Chronic stress can lead to a range of health issues, including high blood pressure, heart disease, and cognitive decline. However, spending time in nature has been shown to be an effective antidote to the negative effects of stress. Nature promotes relaxation and calms the mind by lowering levels of cortisol, the body's primary stress hormone.

How Nature Reduces Stress:

• **Cortisol Reduction:** *Studies show that spending time in natural environments reduces cortisol levels, which helps mitigate the physical effects of stress.*

• **Calming Effect:** *Natural settings provide a peaceful environment that promotes relaxation, helping to reduce anxiety and improve overall well-being.*

• **Connection to the Present Moment:** *Nature helps to ground us in the present moment, which encourages mindfulness and reduces rumination and stress-induced negative thinking.*

• **Improved Mental Clarity:** *Nature's calming effect allows the brain to rest and rejuvenate, improving focus and mental clarity when you return to daily tasks.*

2. Nature's Impact on Mental Health

Beyond reducing stress, exposure to nature has profound benefits for mental health. People who spend more time outdoors report lower levels of depression, anxiety, and mental fatigue. Nature can also have therapeutic effects on individuals suffering from mental health disorders, helping to improve mood, cognitive function, and emotional stability.

Mental Health Benefits of Nature:

• **Reduced Anxiety and Depression:** *Time spent in natural settings has been shown to decrease symptoms of anxiety and depression, improving emotional well-being.*

• **Enhanced Mood:** *Research has found that spending time outdoors increases the production of serotonin and endorphins, which are hormones associated with happiness and improved mood.*

• **Mental Fatigue Recovery:** *Natural environments allow the mind to recharge by reducing cognitive fatigue and promoting mental rejuvenation.*

• **Improved Cognitive Function:** *Regular exposure to nature enhances attention span, memory, and creativity, which supports overall cognitive health.*

Benefits of Sunlight and Fresh Air

1. Sunlight and Vitamin D: A Key for Longevity

Sunlight is a natural source of Vitamin D, which is essential for various bodily functions, including calcium absorption, immune system support, and bone health. Vitamin D deficiency has been linked to numerous health issues, including weakened bones, immune dysfunction, and even chronic diseases. Getting sunlight regularly can help ensure you maintain healthy Vitamin D levels, which are vital for longevity.

How Sunlight Supports Health:

• **Vitamin D Production:** *When your skin is exposed to sunlight, it produces Vitamin D, which supports bone health, reduces inflammation, and boosts immune function.*

• **Boosts Mood and Energy:** *Sunlight helps regulate the production of serotonin, which can boost your mood, reduce feelings of anxiety, and increase energy levels.*

• **Improved Sleep Quality:** *Sunlight exposure during the day helps regulate your circadian rhythm, leading to better sleep at night. Proper sleep is crucial for overall health and longevity.*

• **Cancer Prevention:** *Some studies suggest that moderate sunlight exposure may reduce the risk of certain cancers, such as breast, prostate, and colon cancer, by improving immune function and Vitamin D production.*

2. The Healing Power of Fresh Air

Fresh air is another essential element of time spent outdoors. The air we breathe plays a significant role in our overall health, affecting everything from lung function to mental clarity. Spending time outdoors in nature provides cleaner, fresher air than the indoor environments many of us inhabit, which can be filled with pollutants and toxins.

Health Benefits of Fresh Air:

• **Improved Respiratory Function:** *Fresh air contains higher levels of oxygen, which can enhance lung function and overall respiratory health.*

• **Enhanced Blood Circulation:** *The higher oxygen levels found outdoors promote better circulation and heart health.*

• **Reduced Toxic Exposure:** *Time outdoors helps minimize exposure to indoor pollutants, such as chemicals from cleaning products, allergens, and secondhand smoke.*

• **Boosted Immune System:** *Fresh air helps increase the oxygen supply to the body's cells, improving overall immune function and boosting the body's ability to fight infections.*

Practical Ways to Incorporate Nature into Your Life

1. Outdoor Exercise and Movement

One of the best ways to harness the benefits of nature is to incorporate outdoor physical activities into your daily routine. Whether it's walking, hiking, cycling, or yoga in the park, outdoor exercise combines the health benefits of physical activity with the healing effects of nature.

Ideas for Outdoor Exercise:

• **Walking or Hiking:** *Walking or hiking in a park, forest, or nature reserve can provide both physical exercise and the calming effects of nature.*

• **Yoga and Tai Chi:** *These mindful practices can be especially rejuvenating when practiced outdoors, connecting the mind, body, and nature.*

• **Cycling or Running:** *Cycling and running outdoors expose you to fresh air and sunlight while providing cardiovascular benefits.*

• **Gardening:** *Gardening is a physically engaging outdoor activity that allows you to interact with nature, promote mental clarity, and reduce stress.*

2. Spending Time in Nature Daily

Even if you can't spend hours outdoors each day, incorporating small amounts of nature into your routine can still provide significant benefits. Whether it's a short walk in the park, sitting outside with a book, or simply enjoying your morning coffee on a balcony, connecting with nature, even briefly, can have a positive impact on your health.

Simple Ways to Connect with Nature:

• **Morning Walks:** *Start your day with a walk in a natural area to boost energy levels and set a calm tone for the day.*

• **Picnics and Outdoor Meals:** *Enjoy meals outside, even if it's just in your garden or on your balcony, to combine nourishment with nature's therapeutic effects.*

• **Bring Nature Indoors:** *Surround yourself with indoor plants, open windows for fresh air, or place nature-inspired art around your home to bring the outdoors inside.*

Nature as a Lifelong Partner in Health

Nature offers an abundant source of healing and rejuvenation that is free and accessible to everyone. Time spent outdoors, whether through physical activity, relaxation, or simply enjoying the natural world, contributes to improved stress management, better mental health, and enhanced physical well-being. Sunlight and fresh air are vital for optimal health and longevity, supporting everything from immune function to mental clarity.

By incorporating nature into your daily life, you can experience the profound benefits of outdoor time and tap into nature's healing power to support a longer, healthier, and more vibrant life.

CHAPTER 18
ELIMINATING TOXINS

Toxins are a significant factor that can accelerate the aging process and negatively impact overall health. In this chapter, we will explore how to reduce exposure to harmful substances such as pollutants, alcohol, and smoking, as well as how to detoxify your environment to promote long-term wellness and longevity. The aim is to empower you with the knowledge and practical steps to create a cleaner, healthier life, free from the toxins that can rob you of vitality and well-being.

Reducing Exposure to Pollutants, Alcohol, and Smoking

1. The Dangers of Environmental Pollutants

Environmental pollutants, such as air pollution, chemicals in the water, and toxins in our food, can contribute to a wide range of health issues, including respiratory problems, cardiovascular disease, and even cancer. These pollutants also increase oxidative stress in the body, which accelerates aging and increases the risk of chronic disease.

How Pollutants Affect the Body:

• **Air Pollution:** *Exposure to polluted air, particularly fine particulate matter (PM2.5), has been linked to respiratory diseases, heart disease, and premature aging. Long-term exposure can cause inflammation in the lungs and heart, leading to chronic conditions.*

• **Toxic Chemicals in Water:** *Water contamination, often with heavy metals like lead and mercury, pesticides, and industrial chemicals, can have serious health implications, from kidney damage to neurotoxicity.*

• **Pesticides and Herbicides in Food:** *Many conventionally grown foods contain pesticide residues, which may disrupt hormonal balance, impair immune function, and contribute to the development of certain cancers.*

2. Reducing Alcohol Consumption

While moderate alcohol consumption may have some social benefits, excessive drinking is known to damage the liver, increase the risk of cardiovascular disease, weaken the immune system, and accelerate aging. Alcohol disrupts sleep, impairs cognitive function, and dehydrates the body, leading to a reduction in both physical and mental well-being over time.

How Alcohol Affects Health:

• **Liver Damage:** *Chronic alcohol consumption leads to fatty liver disease, cirrhosis, and even liver cancer. The liver's detoxification capabilities are impaired when overwhelmed by alcohol.*

• **Cognitive Impairment:** *Long-term alcohol use is associated with cognitive decline, memory loss, and an increased risk of Alzheimer's and dementia.*

• **Accelerated Aging:** *Alcohol dehydrates the skin, causing wrinkles and fine lines to appear more quickly. It also disrupts the body's ability to repair damaged cells and tissues, contributing to accelerated aging.*

• **Immune Suppression:** *Excessive alcohol weakens the immune system, making the body more susceptible to infections and illnesses.*

3. The Harmful Effects of Smoking

Smoking is one of the most significant contributors to premature aging, with the harmful effects extending to nearly every organ in the body. Smoking damages the skin, accelerates aging, and increases the risk of numerous life-threatening conditions, including heart disease, lung cancer, and chronic obstructive pulmonary disease (COPD).

How Smoking Accelerates Aging:

• **Premature Wrinkling:** *Smoking constricts blood vessels, reducing blood flow to the skin, leading to a lack of oxygen and nutrients and the early appearance of wrinkles and sagging.*

• **Increased Inflammation:** *The toxins in cigarette smoke promote inflammation throughout the body, contributing to chronic diseases and faster cellular aging.*

• **Reduced Healing Ability:** *Smoking impairs the body's ability to repair itself, slowing down wound healing and tissue regeneration.*

• **Increased Cancer Risk:** *Smoking is a leading cause of various cancers, including lung, throat, mouth, and bladder cancer. The carcinogens in tobacco damage DNA, leading to mutations and the development of cancerous cells.*

Detoxifying Your Environment

1. Creating a Toxin-Free Home

Your home is where you spend a significant amount of time, so it is essential to make it a safe, clean, and healthy environment. Many common household products, such as cleaning supplies, air fresheners, and furniture, can contain harmful chemicals that contribute to indoor air pollution and toxin exposure. Detoxifying your living space is an important step in reducing the overall toxin load on your body.

How to Detoxify Your Home:

- **Air Purifiers:** *Invest in air purifiers with HEPA filters to remove fine particles, allergens, and pollutants from the air. Regularly open windows to increase ventilation and reduce the buildup of indoor air toxins.*

- **Non-Toxic Cleaning Products:** *Replace harsh chemical-based cleaning products with natural alternatives like vinegar, baking soda, and lemon. Use essential oils for natural fragrances instead of synthetic air fresheners.*

- **Avoid Flame Retardants:** *Flame retardants are often found in furniture and textiles, but they contain chemicals that can accumulate in the body and increase the risk of hormonal disruption and cancer. Look for flame-retardant-free furniture.*

- **Indoor Plants:** *Certain indoor plants, such as spider plants, peace lilies, and snake plants, can help purify the air by absorbing toxins and releasing oxygen.*

- **Natural Fabrics and Materials:** *Opt for organic cotton, wool, or linen in your bedding, furniture, and clothing to avoid exposure to synthetic chemicals used in conventional manufacturing processes.*

2. Detoxifying the Body

Aside from removing toxins from your environment, it's essential to support your body's own detoxification processes. The body has its natural detox systems, including the liver, kidneys, and lymphatic system, but a healthy lifestyle can help support and enhance their function.

Ways to Support Detoxification:

- **Hydration:** *Drinking plenty of water is essential for flushing out toxins and maintaining kidney function. Water helps dilute and expel harmful substances from the body through urine.*

- **Fiber-Rich Foods:** *Eating a diet rich in fiber from fruits, vegetables, and whole grains supports the digestive system and promotes the elimina-*

tion of waste products. Fiber binds to toxins in the digestive tract and helps expel them through the intestines.

• **Liver Support:** *Foods like garlic, cruciferous vegetables (broccoli, cauliflower, kale), and beets help support liver function and detoxification.*

• **Sweating:** *Regular exercise, saunas, and hot baths promote sweating, which helps the body eliminate toxins through the skin.*

• **Dry Brushing:** *Using a natural bristle brush to gently exfoliate the skin can stimulate the lymphatic system and encourage toxin elimination through the skin.*

3. Reducing Chemical Exposure in Personal Care Products

Many personal care products, such as shampoos, lotions, and cosmetics, contain synthetic chemicals that can be absorbed through the skin and accumulate in the body over time. Switching to natural or organic personal care products can reduce your toxin exposure.

Tips for Detoxifying Personal Care Products:

• **Choose Natural Brands:** *Look for personal care products labeled "organic" or "natural" and avoid those with synthetic fragrances, parabens, sulfates, and phthalates.*

• **Use Essential Oils:** *Essential oils can replace many synthetic fragrances found in perfumes and lotions. They also offer therapeutic benefits for the skin and mood.*

• **Make Your Own Products:** *Consider making your own skincare products using natural ingredients like coconut oil, honey, and aloe vera.*

Creating a Toxin-Free, Longevity-Focused Lifestyle

Eliminating toxins from your life is an essential step in living a longer, healthier life. By reducing exposure to environmental pollutants, avoiding harmful substances like alcohol and smoking, and detoxifying your home and body, you can significantly improve your overall health and longevity. Creating a cleaner environment, both internally and externally, helps your body function at its best, protecting you from the harmful effects of toxins and promoting long-term well-being.

Incorporating these strategies into your daily life will not only help you feel more vibrant and energized but also increase your chances of enjoying a long, healthy, and fulfilling life.

CHAPTER 19

THE GENETICS OF LONGEVITY

When it comes to longevity, many people wonder how much of it is determined by their genetics. Are we destined to live long lives based solely on the genes we inherit from our parents, or can lifestyle choices play a significant role? In this chapter, we'll explore the genetic factors that contribute to longevity, as well as the emerging field of epigenetics, which demonstrates how our lifestyle choices can alter the way our genes express themselves.

How Much of Longevity is Inherited?

Genetics undoubtedly plays a role in determining how long we live, but it is not the sole factor. Studies have shown that around 20-30% of an individual's lifespan can be attributed to their genetic makeup, while the remaining 70-80% is influenced by lifestyle, environment, and behavioral factors.

Genetic Factors Linked to Longevity:

·**The Role of Telomeres:** Telomeres are protective caps at the ends of chromosomes that shorten as we age. Some people are born with longer telomeres, which may slow down the aging process. Genetic factors that influence telomere length have been linked to longevity, as individuals with longer telomeres tend to live longer and have a lower risk of age-related diseases.

·**Longevity Genes:** Certain genes have been found to correlate with increased lifespan. These include the **FOXO3 gene**, which has been linked to longevity in various populations, and the **APOE gene**, which is associated with reduced risk of Alzheimer's disease. Variants of the **SIRT1** gene, involved in regulating the body's response to stress and aging, are also believed to contribute to a longer life.

·**Inherited Disease Resistance:** Some genetic traits provide resistance to diseases that can shorten lifespan, such as cardiovascular disease, cancer, and diabetes. People who inherit genetic variants that protect against these diseases may have an advantage when it comes to living a long life.

While these genetic traits contribute to longevity, they are not an automatic guarantee of a long life. Instead, they create a foundation upon which lifestyle choices can either enhance or detract from the potential for longevity.

Epigenetics: Changing Gene Expression Through Lifestyle

While our genetic blueprint provides the foundation for our biology, **epigenetics** refers to the study of how our lifestyle choices and environmental factors can influence the way our genes are expressed. Unlike genetic mutations, which involve changes to the DNA sequence itself, epigenetic changes can modify gene activity without altering the underlying DNA code.

Epigenetic modifications can turn genes "on" or "off," influencing how the body responds to aging, stress, inflammation, and disease. This concept is crucial because it suggests that our lifestyle choices —such as diet, exercise, sleep, and stress management—can actively impact how our genes express themselves, potentially enhancing longevity and healthspan.

Key Epigenetic Mechanisms:

1.**DNA Methylation:** One of the most studied epigenetic mechanisms, DNA methylation involves adding a methyl group to DNA, which can silence certain genes. Lifestyle factors like diet, exercise, and stress levels can influence DNA methylation patterns, potentially turning on genes that protect against age-related diseases or turning off genes that contribute to aging and disease development.

2.**Histone Modification:** Histones are proteins that help organize DNA in the cell nucleus. Chemical modifications to histones can change how tightly or loosely DNA is wrapped around them, affecting gene expression. Proper lifestyle habits, such as physical activity and balanced nutrition, can positively influence histone modifications, potentially leading to longer, healthier lives.

3.**Non-Coding RNA:** These RNA molecules do not code for proteins but play a crucial role in regulating gene expression. Certain lifestyle factors, like maintaining a healthy weight or avoiding toxins, have been shown to impact non-coding RNA activity, which can affect aging processes and disease resistance.

The Role of Lifestyle in Epigenetic Expression

While genetic inheritance sets the stage, epigenetics allows for modification, which means that lifestyle choices can actively influence how our genes express themselves and ultimately impact our longevity. By understanding the science of epigenetics, we can take steps to optimize our health and extend our lifespan.

1. Nutrition: Fueling Your Epigenome

What we eat has a direct impact on our epigenome. Certain foods can trigger beneficial epigenetic changes, while others can have detrimental effects.

• **Fruits and Vegetables:** *Rich in antioxidants, vitamins, and phytochemicals, fruits and vegetables can promote beneficial epigenetic modifi-*

cations that enhance longevity. For instance, compounds like **flavonoids** *and* **polyphenols** *found in berries, green leafy vegetables, and tea are known to affect DNA methylation, helping to regulate genes associated with inflammation and aging.*

• **Omega-3 Fatty Acids:** *Found in fatty fish, flaxseeds, and walnuts, omega-3 fatty acids have been shown to influence DNA methylation and histone modification, which may help reduce the risk of age-related diseases and promote healthy aging.*

• **Polyphenols in Green Tea:** *Green tea contains polyphenols, which have been shown to influence gene expression and reduce oxidative stress, contributing to healthy aging.*

2. Exercise: Reprogramming Your Genes

Physical activity is one of the most powerful ways to influence gene expression and enhance longevity. Exercise has been shown to affect a wide range of epigenetic mechanisms, including DNA methylation and histone modification, to promote health and slow down the aging process.

• **Aerobic Exercise:** *Activities like walking, running, cycling, and swimming can help reduce inflammation and increase the expression of genes involved in mitochondrial function, cardiovascular health, and longevity.*

• **Strength Training:** *Resistance training has been shown to increase muscle mass, improve bone density, and regulate the expression of genes related to muscle repair and growth, thus supporting physical function as we age.*

• **Regular Movement:** *It's also essential to incorporate non-exercise movement, such as walking or stretching, into your daily routine. The combination of exercise and non-exercise physical activity works synergistically to influence gene expression positively.*

3. Sleep: Restoring the Epigenome

Adequate sleep is essential for gene repair and expression. Sleep helps maintain the body's internal balance and ensures the proper functioning of the brain and immune system.

• **Sleep and Epigenetics:** *Studies show that poor sleep can disrupt epigenetic mechanisms that regulate inflammation and repair. Chronic sleep deprivation has been linked to the expression of genes associated with age-related diseases, such as heart disease, diabetes, and cognitive decline.*

• **Optimizing Sleep:** *Ensure seven to nine hours of quality sleep per night by maintaining a regular sleep schedule, creating a restful environment, and practicing good sleep hygiene. This promotes positive epigenetic changes that support longevity.*

4. Stress Management: Epigenetic Control of Inflammation

Chronic stress is a major contributor to aging and disease. Epigenetic mechanisms triggered by stress can accelerate aging by influencing genes associated with inflammation, immune function, and cellular repair.

• **Mindfulness and Meditation:** *Practices like meditation, yoga, and mindfulness have been shown to reverse some of the epigenetic changes associated with chronic stress, reducing inflammation and promoting a healthy gene expression pattern that supports longevity.*

• **Social Connection:** *Strong social bonds have been linked to positive epigenetic changes that reduce stress and promote better health outcomes.*

Embracing Your Epigenetic Potential

While genetics provide the blueprint for our lives, epigenetics reveals the exciting potential for modifying that blueprint through lifestyle choices. By understanding how nutrition, exercise, sleep, and stress management influence gene expression, we can take control of our health and longevity.

Incorporating practices that promote beneficial epigenetic changes, such as eating a nutrient-rich diet, engaging in regular physical activity, prioritizing sleep, and managing stress, allows us to optimize our genetic potential and live longer, healthier lives. Embrace the power of epigenetics to shape your longevity journey and maximize your healthspan.

CHAPTER 20
HORMONES AND AGING

Hormones play a crucial role in regulating many of the body's vital functions, including metabolism, mood, energy, and reproductive health. As we age, hormonal changes can significantly impact our health and well-being. In this chapter, we'll explore how balancing key hormones can support vitality and longevity, the common signs of hormonal imbalance, and strategies for optimizing hormone levels to promote healthy aging.

Balancing Key Hormones for Vitality

Our hormone levels fluctuate throughout life, with significant changes occurring as we enter different stages of aging. These fluctuations can affect energy, muscle mass, bone density, skin elasticity, mental clarity, and even our emotional health. By understanding how to balance key hormones, we can help mitigate some of the negative effects of aging and support a more vibrant, energetic life.

1. Estrogen and Progesterone (In Women)

For women, the decline in estrogen and progesterone during menopause is one of the most significant hormonal changes they will experience. These hormones are crucial for regulating the menstrual cycle, maintaining bone density, supporting cardiovascular health, and preserving skin elasticity.

·**Estrogen:** As estrogen levels drop during menopause, women may experience symptoms such as hot flashes, mood swings, sleep disturbances, and vaginal dryness. Estrogen also plays a role in maintaining bone density, and its decline can lead to osteoporosis.

·**Progesterone:** This hormone works in tandem with estrogen to regulate the menstrual cycle. As progesterone levels drop, women may experience irregular periods, irritability, and even increased anxiety.

Balancing Estrogen and Progesterone:

• **Dietary Support:** *Foods like soy, flaxseeds, and cruciferous vegetables contain compounds that can help balance estrogen levels. These foods provide phytoestrogens, which are plant-based compounds that mimic estrogen in the body.*

• **Lifestyle Factors:** *Regular exercise, particularly strength training and aerobic exercises, can help balance hormones by reducing stress and inflammation. Managing stress through mindfulness, yoga, or deep-breathing exercises can also support hormonal balance.*

• **Bioidentical Hormone Therapy (BHT):** *For some women, bioidentical hormone replacement therapy (BHRT) may be considered to address the symptoms of menopause and restore hormonal balance. It's important to consult with a healthcare provider before considering this option.*

2. Testosterone (In Both Men and Women)

Testosterone is often associated with men, but women also produce testosterone in smaller amounts. In both men and women, testosterone plays a key role in maintaining muscle mass, bone density, energy levels, mood, and libido. As we age, testosterone levels tend to decline, which can contribute to the loss of muscle mass, fatigue, and diminished sexual desire.

· **In Men:** Testosterone levels naturally decrease with age, typically starting after the age of 30. Low testosterone in men, a condition sometimes referred to as "low T," can result in symptoms such as fatigue, depression, decreased muscle mass, and low libido.

· **In Women:** Testosterone levels also decline in women as they age, particularly after menopause. This can contribute to a loss of energy, reduced sexual drive, and difficulty building muscle mass.

Balancing Testosterone:

• **Exercise:** *Strength training and high-intensity interval training (HIIT) are particularly effective in boosting testosterone levels. Regular exercise also helps maintain muscle mass and supports overall vitality.*

• **Nutrition:** *Eating a balanced diet rich in healthy fats (like those from avocados, nuts, and olive oil) and adequate protein helps optimize testosterone production. Zinc-rich foods, such as oysters, beans, and pumpkin seeds, are also important for maintaining healthy testosterone levels.*

• **Sleep:** *Poor sleep can lower testosterone levels, so getting adequate rest is essential for maintaining healthy hormone levels.*

3. Thyroid Hormones

The thyroid gland produces hormones that regulate metabolism, energy production, and temperature control. As we age, thyroid dysfunction can become more common. An underactive thyroid (hypothyroidism) can lead to fatigue, weight gain, depression, and a slow metabolism, while an overactive thyroid (hyperthyroidism) can cause weight loss, anxiety, and heart palpitations.

Signs of Thyroid Imbalance:

• **Hypothyroidism (Low Thyroid):** *Symptoms include fatigue, weight gain, constipation, dry skin, and hair loss.*

• **Hyperthyroidism (High Thyroid):** *Symptoms include rapid heart rate, weight loss, irritability, sweating, and increased appetite.*

Balancing Thyroid Hormones:

• **Dietary Support:** *Iodine, selenium, and zinc are essential for healthy thyroid function. Seaweed, eggs, and Brazil nuts are good sources of these nutrients.*

• **Avoiding Endocrine Disruptors:** *Chemicals like BPA, phthalates, and parabens, found in plastics and personal care products, can interfere with thyroid function. Limiting exposure to these chemicals is key for maintaining healthy thyroid levels.*

• **Thyroid Hormone Replacement Therapy (HRT):** *For those with hypothyroidism, thyroid hormone replacement therapy, such as levothyroxine, can help restore proper thyroid function. It is essential to consult with a healthcare provider for proper testing and treatment.*

4. Insulin and Blood Sugar Regulation

Insulin is a hormone produced by the pancreas that regulates blood sugar levels. As we age, insulin sensitivity may decrease, leading to insulin resistance, a condition in which the body becomes less responsive to insulin. This can lead to elevated blood sugar levels and, if left unchecked, may contribute to the development of type 2 diabetes and metabolic syndrome.

Signs of Insulin Imbalance:

• **Insulin Resistance:** *Symptoms may include increased hunger, weight gain, fatigue, and difficulty losing weight.*

• **Blood Sugar Spikes:** *High blood sugar levels may lead to frequent urination, excessive thirst, and blurred vision.*

Balancing Insulin:

• **Diet:** *Eating a low-glycemic, whole-foods-based diet can help stabilize blood sugar levels. Emphasize foods with a low glycemic index, such as whole grains, legumes, and non-starchy vegetables, and reduce consumption of refined sugars and processed foods.*

• **Intermittent Fasting:** *Intermittent fasting can improve insulin sensitivity by allowing the body to rest from constant food intake, promoting better blood sugar regulation.*

• **Exercise:** *Physical activity, particularly strength training and aerobic exercises, helps improve insulin sensitivity and manage blood sugar levels.*

5. Cortisol: The Stress Hormone

Cortisol is a hormone produced by the adrenal glands in response to stress. While cortisol is essential for regulating the body's stress response, chronic stress can lead to elevated cortisol levels, which in turn can interfere with other hormones, impair immune function, and increase the risk of heart disease. Over time, consistently high cortisol levels can accelerate aging.

Signs of Cortisol Imbalance:

• **High Cortisol:** *Symptoms include weight gain, particularly around the abdomen, anxiety, insomnia, high blood pressure, and a weakened immune system.*

• **Low Cortisol:** *Symptoms include fatigue, low blood pressure, dizziness, and a lack of motivation.*

Balancing Cortisol:

• **Stress Management:** *Practices such as mindfulness meditation, yoga, deep breathing, and progressive muscle relaxation can help lower cortisol levels and promote relaxation.*

• **Sleep:** *Prioritizing quality sleep is essential for managing cortisol levels. Chronic sleep deprivation can lead to an overproduction of cortisol.*

• **Physical Activity:** *Regular physical activity, particularly moderate-intensity exercise like walking, swimming, or cycling, can help lower cortisol levels over time.*

Signs of Hormonal Imbalance

Hormonal imbalances often manifest through various physical and emotional symptoms. Understanding these signs can help you recognize when something might be off and take proactive steps to balance your hormones:

- **Fatigue and Low Energy**

- **Mood Swings and Irritability**

- **Changes in Sleep Patterns**

- **Weight Gain or Difficulty Losing Weight**

- **Reduced Libido**

- **Hair Loss or Thinning**

- **Brain Fog or Poor Memory**

- **Changes in Skin Elasticity and Appearance**

Optimizing Hormones for Healthy Aging

Hormonal balance is crucial for maintaining vitality, health, and longevity. As we age, hormonal fluctuations are natural, but the way we manage these changes can significantly impact how we feel and function. By supporting our body's natural hormonal rhythms through proper diet, exercise, stress management, and, when necessary, medical interventions, we can optimize our hormone levels and enhance our quality of life as we age.

Understanding your hormones and taking steps to balance them can help you live with more energy, clarity, and strength, allowing you to enjoy a longer, healthier life. Always consult with a healthcare provider before making major changes or starting hormone therapies to ensure a personalized and safe approach to hormonal health.

CHAPTER 21

MONITORING YOUR HEALTH METRICS

One of the most important aspects of maintaining a long, healthy life is staying on top of your health by regularly monitoring key metrics and biomarkers. As we age, our bodies undergo natural changes that can affect our overall health. Regularly checking certain health metrics allows us to catch potential issues early and take proactive steps to prevent or manage chronic conditions, ensuring a longer, more vibrant life. In this chapter, we'll explore the key biomarkers you should track, how they influence your longevity, and the importance of regular checkups in managing your health over time.

Key Biomarkers for Longevity

Biomarkers are measurable indicators of biological processes or conditions in the body. Monitoring these biomarkers can give us valuable insight into our overall health and provide early warnings of potential health risks. The following key biomarkers are particularly important for assessing long-term health and longevity:

1. Cholesterol Levels

Cholesterol is a fatty substance found in your blood that plays an important role in building cells and producing certain hormones.

However, when cholesterol levels are too high, it can lead to the buildup of fatty deposits in your arteries, increasing the risk of heart disease, stroke, and other cardiovascular conditions.

- **Key Measurements:**

◦ **Total Cholesterol:** *This is the overall amount of cholesterol in your blood, including both HDL (good cholesterol) and LDL (bad cholesterol). Ideally, total cholesterol should be less than 200 mg/dL.*

◦ **LDL (Low-Density Lipoprotein):** *Often referred to as "bad" cholesterol, high LDL levels can lead to plaque buildup in arteries. The recommended level is less than 100 mg/dL.*

◦ **HDL (High-Density Lipoprotein):** *Known as "good" cholesterol, HDL helps remove LDL cholesterol from the bloodstream. A higher HDL level (above 60 mg/dL) is protective against heart disease.*

◦ **Triglycerides:** *These are another type of fat in the blood. High triglyceride levels (over 150 mg/dL) can increase the risk of heart disease.*

Why It's Important:

Tracking cholesterol levels is crucial for preventing heart disease and maintaining cardiovascular health. Elevated LDL or triglycerides can increase the risk of heart attacks and strokes, while high HDL can offer protection.

How to Manage It:

- **Diet:** *Eating a heart-healthy diet rich in fiber, healthy fats (like those from olive oil, avocados, and fatty fish), and low in saturated and trans fats can help lower LDL levels and raise HDL levels.*

- **Exercise:** *Regular physical activity, especially aerobic exercise, can help improve your cholesterol profile by increasing HDL and lowering LDL.*

- **Medication:** *If cholesterol levels are significantly high, statins or other medications may be prescribed by a healthcare provider to lower LDL cholesterol.*

2. Inflammation Levels

Chronic inflammation is a silent contributor to many age-related diseases, including heart disease, diabetes, Alzheimer's disease, and even cancer. While inflammation is a natural immune response, long-term or excessive inflammation can damage tissues and organs, accelerating the aging process.

- **Key Biomarkers for Inflammation:**

  ○ **C-Reactive Protein (CRP):** *CRP is a protein produced by the liver in response to inflammation. Elevated levels of CRP are associated with an increased risk of heart disease and other inflammatory conditions.*

  ○ **Fibrinogen:** *Another protein produced in response to inflammation, fibrinogen helps with blood clotting. High levels of fibrinogen are linked to cardiovascular disease.*

  ○ **Interleukin-6 (IL-6):** *This pro-inflammatory cytokine is elevated in chronic inflammation and has been associated with several chronic diseases.*

Why It's Important:

Chronic low-grade inflammation can contribute to the development of many diseases, including heart disease, diabetes, and neurodegenerative conditions like Alzheimer's. Keeping inflammation levels in check can reduce the risk of these age-related diseases.

How to Manage It:

- **Anti-Inflammatory Diet:** *A diet rich in antioxidant-rich foods, omega-3 fatty acids, and polyphenols (found in berries, leafy greens, nuts, and fatty fish) can help reduce inflammation. Avoid processed foods, refined sugars, and excessive alcohol, all of which can promote inflammation.*

- **Exercise:** *Regular physical activity helps reduce inflammatory markers by promoting healthy blood flow and improving immune system function.*

• **Stress Reduction:** *Chronic stress is a major driver of inflammation. Mindfulness practices, yoga, meditation, and other stress-reduction techniques can help lower inflammation levels.*

3. Blood Sugar and Insulin Sensitivity

Blood sugar (glucose) is the body's primary source of energy, but when blood sugar levels are consistently high, it can lead to insulin resistance, diabetes, and other metabolic disorders. Insulin is the hormone responsible for helping cells take in glucose from the bloodstream. Over time, insulin resistance can result in higher blood sugar levels, increasing the risk of chronic diseases.

• **Key Measurements:**

◦ **Fasting Blood Sugar:** *This test measures your blood sugar levels after an overnight fast. A healthy range is typically between 70-100 mg/dL. Higher levels may indicate prediabetes or diabetes.*

◦ **Hemoglobin A1c (HbA1c):** *This test measures your average blood sugar levels over the past two to three months. An A1c level of 5.7% to 6.4% indicates prediabetes, while 6.5% or higher suggests diabetes.*

◦ **Insulin Sensitivity:** *Insulin sensitivity refers to how well your body responds to insulin. Poor insulin sensitivity (insulin resistance) can lead to higher blood sugar levels and is a precursor to type 2 diabetes.*

Why It's Important:

Maintaining healthy blood sugar levels and insulin sensitivity is key to preventing type 2 diabetes, metabolic syndrome, and other chronic conditions that can impact longevity. Chronic high blood sugar accelerates aging by increasing oxidative stress and inflammation in the body.

How to Manage It:

• **Balanced Diet:** *Focus on a diet with a low glycemic index, including whole grains, legumes, vegetables, and healthy fats, while limiting refined sugars and processed carbs.*

• **Exercise:** *Physical activity improves insulin sensitivity by increasing glucose uptake into muscles and tissues. Strength training and aerobic exercises are particularly beneficial.*

• **Intermittent Fasting:** *Intermittent fasting or time-restricted eating can help improve insulin sensitivity and lower blood sugar levels.*

The Importance of Regular Checkups

While monitoring key biomarkers on your own is important, regular checkups with your healthcare provider are essential for a comprehensive understanding of your health. Routine checkups allow for early detection of potential health issues and provide an opportunity to discuss any changes in your health with a professional.

Why Regular Checkups Matter:

• **Early Detection of Chronic Diseases:** *Regular blood tests and screenings can identify issues like high cholesterol, diabetes, and high blood pressure before symptoms appear, allowing for early intervention.*

• **Personalized Health Plan:** *Your healthcare provider can offer tailored recommendations based on your specific biomarkers, lifestyle, and family history, ensuring a personalized approach to your health and longevity.*

• **Prevention and Maintenance:** *Preventive care, such as vaccinations, cancer screenings, and other health assessments, can help catch issues early and ensure that you are taking the right steps to stay healthy.*

• **Mental Health Check:** *Regular checkups provide an opportunity to discuss mental health concerns, including stress, anxiety, and depression, which can impact overall well-being.*

What to Discuss During Regular Checkups:

• *Review your key biomarkers, including cholesterol, blood sugar, and inflammation levels.*

• *Discuss any new symptoms or changes in your health.*

- *Ask about preventive screenings based on your age, family history, and lifestyle.*

- *Address mental health concerns and stress management strategies.*

Tracking Your Health for a Longer, Healthier Life

Monitoring key health metrics like cholesterol levels, inflammation, and blood sugar is an essential part of maintaining a long, healthy life. These biomarkers provide valuable insights into the state of your health and help you make informed decisions about your lifestyle, diet, and medical care. By regularly tracking your health metrics and attending routine checkups, you can stay ahead of potential health issues, optimize your wellness, and ensure a longer, more vibrant life.

Remember, small changes over time can lead to significant improvements in your health. Prioritize regular monitoring, adopt a balanced lifestyle, and work with healthcare professionals to tailor a plan that supports your long-term health and longevity.

CHAPTER 22
BUILDING RESILIENCE

Resilience is the ability to adapt to adversity, recover from setbacks, and bounce back stronger from challenges—whether physical, emotional, or mental. As we age, the ability to stay resilient becomes even more important, as we may face greater health challenges, life transitions, or unexpected setbacks. Building resilience is not just about enduring hardship, but also about growing stronger and more capable through adversity. This chapter will explore how to cultivate resilience, how the mind and body work together in recovery, and how to foster a resilient mindset for long-term health and longevity.

How to Bounce Back from Illness or Setbacks

Life is full of ups and downs, and at some point, everyone will experience some form of setback—whether it's a physical illness, emotional hardship, or unexpected life event. Resilience isn't about avoiding these difficulties; it's about how we face them, recover, and move forward. Here are key strategies for bouncing back from setbacks:

1. Embrace a Growth Mindset

A growth mindset is the belief that our abilities, intelligence, and even our emotional responses can grow and improve with effort and persistence. Cultivating this mindset can help us see challenges as opportunities for personal growth rather than obstacles.

• **Shift from "Why is this happening to me?" to "What can I learn from this?"**

• *Understand that setbacks are a natural part of life, and how you respond can shape your future well-being.*

Benefits of a Growth Mindset for Resilience:

• *Increased ability to recover from setbacks.*

• *Greater self-efficacy and belief in your ability to improve.*

• *Reduced anxiety and stress in the face of challenges.*

2. Practice Self-Compassion

Resilience doesn't mean ignoring your emotions or pretending you're unaffected by hardship. In fact, being kind to yourself during difficult times can significantly boost your ability to recover. Self-compassion involves treating yourself with the same under-standing and kindness you would offer to a friend in need.

• **How to Practice Self-Compassion:**

◦ *Acknowledge your pain or frustration without judgment.*

◦ *Speak to yourself kindly, without harsh self-criticism.*

◦ *Take breaks when you need them to recharge emotionally and physically.*

Self-compassion fosters emotional resilience, allowing you to bounce back more quickly from setbacks and face future challenges with greater strength.

3. Build a Strong Support System

Having a network of supportive people is one of the strongest contributors to resilience. Whether it's family, friends, or a community, knowing you have people to lean on when times get tough can provide emotional strength and perspective.

• How to Build a Support System:

◦ *Foster deep, meaningful connections with those who uplift you.*

◦ *Don't hesitate to ask for help or share your feelings when you need to.*

◦ *Surround yourself with people who have a positive outlook and who encourage personal growth.*

Having a strong support system helps you recover more quickly, provides a sense of belonging, and reminds you that you are not alone in facing life's challenges.

The Mind-Body Connection in Recovery

The process of recovery involves both physical and emotional healing. The mind and body are deeply interconnected, and strengthening one can help the other. Understanding how the mind-body connection works can help you recover more effectively and build resilience after setbacks.

1. The Role of the Brain in Recovery

The brain plays a critical role in the way we experience and recover from setbacks. Neuroplasticity, the brain's ability to reorganize itself by forming new neural connections, means that we can rewire our brains through positive thinking, emotional regulation, and new experiences.

• Positive Thinking and Resilience:

◦ *Optimistic thinking can reduce stress and help you approach recovery with a sense of hope.*

◦ *Mindfulness and meditation practices have been shown to change brain structures associated with resilience, such as the prefrontal cortex, which governs decision-making and emotional regulation.*

2. The Importance of Emotional Regulation

Emotions are powerful forces in our recovery. When we experience emotional pain, whether from illness, loss, or disappointment, it can feel overwhelming. Learning how to regulate emotions—whether through mindfulness, journaling, or therapy—can prevent emotional turbulence from hindering recovery.

• Mindfulness for Emotional Resilience:

◦ *Mindfulness practices help you stay grounded in the present moment, reducing anxiety and fostering emotional regulation.*

◦ *Techniques such as deep breathing and body scanning can calm the nervous system, promoting recovery and well-being.*

3. Physical Recovery and the Body's Healing Power

The body is incredibly resilient. In fact, the body has its own natural ability to heal itself after injury or illness, as long as we provide the right environment. Proper nutrition, adequate sleep, physical activity, and stress management are essential components of physical recovery.

· Rest and Sleep:

◦ *Sleep is one of the most powerful tools for recovery, as it supports the body's repair processes. Aim for 7–9 hours of restorative sleep each night to help your body regenerate and heal.*

· Movement and Exercise:

◦ *Regular physical activity not only strengthens the body but also helps release endorphins, chemicals in the brain that improve mood and reduce pain.*

◦ *Gentle exercises like yoga or walking can aid in recovery, improving flexibility and reducing the risk of long-term physical limitations.*

· **Nutrition:**

◦ *A nutrient-dense diet rich in antioxidants, healthy fats, and lean proteins supports both physical and mental recovery. Foods rich in omega-3s (like salmon and flaxseeds) can reduce inflammation, while protein helps rebuild tissue and muscle.*

◦ *Hydration is also key—adequate water intake supports the body's healing processes and helps maintain energy levels during recovery.*

Building Resilience Through Lifestyle Habits

To build long-term resilience, it's important to cultivate certain habits that support both the body and mind. These habits can help you bounce back from adversity and strengthen your ability to handle future challenges with grace and fortitude.

1. Regular Exercise

As mentioned earlier, exercise is crucial for both physical and emotional resilience. Not only does it keep the body strong, but it also supports mental health by boosting mood and reducing anxiety. Consistent movement improves circulation, supports the immune system, and builds endurance to help you weather future challenges.

• **Exercise Recommendations:**

◦ *Engage in at least 30 minutes of moderate-intensity exercise most days of the week.*

◦ *Include strength training exercises 2–3 times a week to support muscle mass and bone density.*

◦ *Don't forget flexibility training, like yoga or stretching, to maintain joint health and prevent injury.*

2. Balanced Nutrition

A healthy, well-balanced diet is essential for building resilience.

Nutrient-dense foods fuel both the mind and body, providing the energy and support needed for recovery and strength.

• Resilient Diet Principles:

◦ *Focus on whole foods, including vegetables, fruits, whole grains, healthy fats, and lean proteins.*

◦ *Include anti-inflammatory foods like berries, leafy greens, turmeric, and green tea to reduce the impact of stress on the body.*

◦ *Avoid excessive processed foods, sugar, and alcohol, as they can hinder the body's recovery processes and contribute to long-term health issues.*

3. Stress Management and Mindfulness

Stress is an inevitable part of life, but how we manage it plays a critical role in building resilience. Regular practice of mindfulness, meditation, or breathing exercises can help reduce the physiological effects of stress and promote emotional recovery.

• Mindfulness Techniques:

◦ *Practice deep breathing exercises, such as the 4-7-8 technique, to calm the nervous system.*

◦ *Try guided meditation or mindfulness apps to help cultivate a regular meditation practice.*

◦ *Incorporate journaling to process emotions and gain clarity in times of uncertainty.*

Building Resilience for a Long, Healthy Life

Resilience is a skill that can be nurtured and developed over time. By focusing on the mind-body connection, embracing a growth mindset, and building healthy lifestyle habits, you can strengthen your ability to bounce back from setbacks and face life's challenges with greater fortitude. Resilience is not about avoiding adversity, but about learning to adapt, recover, and grow stronger through it.

By building resilience, you not only enhance your ability to cope with illness and setbacks, but you also improve your overall health and longevity. Life's challenges become opportunities for growth, and with each hurdle you overcome, you lay the foundation for a longer, healthier, and more fulfilling life.

CHAPTER 23
THE SCIENCE OF CALORIC RESTRICTION

Caloric restriction (CR) refers to reducing calorie intake without malnutrition, and it has been one of the most studied practices in the quest for longevity. Research, particularly in animals, has shown that reducing caloric intake while maintaining proper nutrition can extend lifespan and improve health outcomes. In this chapter, we'll delve into the science behind caloric restriction, how it influences longevity, and practical ways to apply this principle in daily life without risking undernutrition or other negative effects.

Research on Caloric Restriction and Longevity

The idea of caloric restriction as a potential path to longer life dates back to the early 20th century, but it wasn't until the 1930s that significant scientific attention was given to the concept. Researchers began to notice that animals subjected to caloric restriction lived longer, had fewer diseases, and exhibited delayed aging. Over the years, studies in mice, rats, and monkeys have provided compelling evidence supporting the notion that reducing caloric intake can extend lifespan and improve health.

1. Animal Studies: The Early Discoveries

Animal studies, particularly in rodents, have shown that caloric restriction can result in:

• **Increased lifespan:** *Mice and rats placed on calorie-restricted diets (about 20-40% fewer calories than they would normally consume) have consistently lived longer compared to those on a normal diet.*

• **Healthier aging:** *Caloric restriction reduces the incidence of age-related diseases such as cancer, heart disease, diabetes, and neurodegenerative conditions like Alzheimer's.*

• **Improved metabolic health:** *These animals show better glucose regulation, lower blood pressure, and improved cholesterol profiles, which are all linked to healthy aging.*

2. Human Studies: Limited but Promising Evidence

While studies on humans are still in their early stages, there is growing evidence that caloric restriction may have similar benefits for human health. Long-term studies on calorie restriction in humans, including studies like the CALERIE trial (Comprehensive Assessment of Long-term Effects of Reducing Intake of Energy), have found:

• **Improved biomarkers of aging:** *Participants who reduced their calorie intake by 15% over two years showed improvements in risk factors for heart disease, such as lower cholesterol levels, improved blood sugar control, and reduced inflammation.*

• **Better metabolic health:** *Caloric restriction in humans has been shown to improve insulin sensitivity, reduce oxidative stress, and support cellular repair processes.*

Although humans live much longer than animals like mice and rats, and it's more difficult to measure lifespan extensions in humans over the course of a typical lifespan, the evidence suggests that caloric restriction may hold promise for slowing down the aging process.

How Caloric Restriction Influences Longevity

The science behind caloric restriction and its impact on longevity primarily revolves around the way it affects the body's metabolism, cellular processes, and genetic pathways involved in aging.

1. Impact on Cellular Repair and Autophagy

Caloric restriction activates a process called **autophagy**, which is a vital mechanism for cellular repair and maintenance. During autophagy, the body breaks down and removes damaged or dysfunctional cells and proteins. This process helps rejuvenate cells and reduce the buildup of harmful waste products that can contribute to aging and disease.

• **Autophagy and Longevity:**

◦ *When calorie intake is reduced, cells enter a "repair" mode, prioritizing the removal of damaged components and the synthesis of new, healthy proteins. This leads to healthier tissues, stronger immune function, and greater cellular longevity.*

2. Hormonal Changes: Insulin, IGF-1, and Growth Hormones

Caloric restriction triggers a variety of hormonal changes that are thought to be crucial for its longevity benefits:

• **Reduced Insulin and Insulin-Like Growth Factor (IGF-1):**

◦ *Lower calorie intake leads to reduced insulin levels and IGF-1, a hormone associated with aging and the growth of cancer cells. Both insulin and IGF-1 are linked to the acceleration of age-related diseases. When caloric intake is restricted, these hormones are suppressed, which can slow the aging process and improve metabolic health.*

• **Increased Human Growth Hormone (HGH):**

◦ *Caloric restriction also increases the secretion of human growth hormone (HGH), which plays a role in tissue regeneration, muscle growth, and fat metabolism. Increased HGH levels are linked to improved muscle mass and reduced age-related frailty.*

3. Reduction in Oxidative Stress and Inflammation

Oxidative stress (the damage caused by free radicals) and chronic inflammation are two major contributors to aging and age-related diseases. Caloric restriction has been shown to:

• **Decrease oxidative stress:** *Reducing caloric intake reduces the production of free radicals, thus preventing damage to cells, proteins, and DNA.*

• **Lower inflammation levels:** *Chronic low-grade inflammation is a key driver of aging. Caloric restriction has been shown to reduce inflammatory markers, which may help prevent diseases like heart disease, diabetes, and neurodegeneration.*

4. Activation of Longevity Pathways: Sirtuins and mTOR

Caloric restriction activates various molecular pathways associated with longevity, particularly those involving **sirtuins** and **mTOR** (mechanistic target of rapamycin).

• **Sirtuins:**

◦ *These proteins are involved in regulating cellular health and stress resistance. Caloric restriction activates sirtuins, which helps protect against DNA damage, supports mitochondrial function, and delays the onset of age-related diseases.*

• **mTOR:**

◦ *mTOR is a protein complex involved in regulating growth and metabolism. When calorie intake is reduced, the mTOR pathway is downregulated, leading to a reduction in cell growth and an increase in cell repair, both of which are linked to longer, healthier lives.*

Practical Approaches to Caloric Restriction Without Undernutrition

While the science behind caloric restriction is compelling, the practical application of this approach is essential to ensure it benefits health without causing malnutrition, fatigue, or other negative outcomes. Here are some ways to approach caloric restriction without going to extremes:

1. Moderate Caloric Reduction

Instead of extreme calorie restriction, aim for a moderate reduction in calories, typically around 10-20%. This can be achieved through:

• **Portion control:** *Reduce portion sizes during meals while still enjoying a variety of foods.*

• **Mindful eating:** *Focus on eating nutrient-dense foods rather than cutting out entire food groups. Avoid processed foods and excess sugar, and instead fill your plate with whole foods rich in vitamins, minerals, and antioxidants.*

2. Intermittent Fasting

Intermittent fasting (IF) is a form of eating where you cycle between periods of eating and fasting, usually in a 16-hour fast with an 8-hour eating window. IF has been shown to mimic the effects of caloric restriction, including reduced insulin levels, increased autophagy, and improved metabolic health, without requiring constant calorie reduction.

• **Popular Intermittent Fasting Methods:**

◦ **16:8 Method:** *Fast for 16 hours and eat within an 8-hour window.*

◦ **5:2 Method:** *Eat normally for five days a week and restrict calories to about 500–600 on two non-consecutive days.*

3. Nutrient-Dense Foods

When reducing calories, it's crucial to ensure that your body still receives all the essential nutrients it needs for optimal health. Focus on foods that provide high nutrient density without excessive calories:

• **Leafy greens, vegetables, and fruits** *are packed with vitamins, minerals, and antioxidants.*

• **Whole grains** *like quinoa, brown rice, and oats provide fiber and important nutrients without excess calories.*

• **Lean proteins** *from plant-based sources (beans, lentils, tofu) or healthy animal sources (fish, chicken) help maintain muscle mass and support metabolism.*

4. Focus on Quality, Not Just Quantity

Caloric restriction isn't just about eating less—it's also about eating better. Ensure that every calorie you consume is rich in essential nutrients. This means focusing on whole foods, high-quality fats (like avocados, nuts, and olive oil), plant-based proteins, and antioxidant-rich fruits and vegetables.

The Potential of Caloric Restriction for Longevity

Caloric restriction offers promising insights into how we might extend lifespan and improve health by slowing the aging process and preventing age-related diseases. Although much of the research is still in its early stages, particularly in humans, the evidence supports the idea that reducing calorie intake without malnutrition can have profound health benefits.

By embracing moderate caloric reduction, mindful eating practices, and nutrient-dense foods, we can mimic the benefits of caloric restriction without extreme measures. Intermittent fasting and mindful portion control offer practical, sustainable ways to reduce caloric intake, improve metabolic health, and support longevity.

Ultimately, while caloric restriction is a powerful tool for improving health and longevity, the key to its success lies in finding a balanced approach that supports both the body's nutritional needs and its desire for long-term vitality.

CHAPTER 24
BIOHACKING FOR LONGEVITY

Biohacking is the practice of using science, technology, and lifestyle changes to optimize the body's performance and extend lifespan. In recent years, biohacking for longevity has become increasingly popular, with emerging tools and techniques aimed at improving health, slowing aging, and enhancing mental and physical performance. While some of these methods are groundbreaking, it's essential to strike a balance between cutting-edge biohacking tools and more traditional, natural approaches to longevity. This chapter will explore the science behind biohacking, including tools like red light therapy, cryotherapy, and nootropics, as well as how to integrate these methods with a holistic approach to health.

Emerging Tools for Biohacking Longevity

Biohacking often focuses on optimizing body functions using external tools or technologies. Here are some of the most popular biohacking techniques that claim to improve longevity and enhance health.

1. Red Light Therapy (Photobiomodulation)

Red light therapy, also known as photobiomodulation (PBM), involves the use of low-wavelength red or near-infrared light to stimulate cellular activity. This therapy is non-invasive and has gained significant attention for its potential to promote healing, reduce inflammation, and slow the aging process.

How Red Light Therapy Works:

• *Red light wavelengths penetrate the skin and interact with the mitochondria, the powerhouse of the cell. This stimulates the production of adenosine triphosphate (ATP), which provides energy to the cells.*

• *The increased ATP production promotes cellular repair, enhances tissue regeneration, reduces oxidative stress, and may even improve collagen production, which is critical for skin health and reducing signs of aging.*

Benefits of Red Light Therapy for Longevity:

• **Skin Health:** *Improves skin tone, texture, and reduces wrinkles by stimulating collagen production.*

• **Muscle Recovery:** *Helps accelerate muscle recovery after exercise by reducing inflammation and promoting tissue healing.*

• **Cognitive Function:** *Some studies suggest it may have neuroprotective effects, promoting brain health and improving cognitive function, which is vital for aging individuals.*

• **Pain Relief:** *Reduces inflammation and pain, particularly for conditions like arthritis and joint pain.*

Practical Use:

• *Red light therapy is commonly used through devices like handheld light panels, LED masks, or full-body light beds. For longevity benefits, sessions of about 10–20 minutes a few times a week are often recommended.*

2. Cryotherapy

Cryotherapy involves the exposure of the body to extremely cold temperatures for short periods of time, typically in a cryo-chamber or through localized treatment (like cryo-facials or cryo-pods). This technique has gained popularity in sports medicine for its recovery benefits and is also touted for its potential anti-aging effects.

How Cryotherapy Works:

• *When the body is exposed to extreme cold (usually around -200 to -300°F or -129 to -184°C), it triggers a range of physiological responses. The body constricts blood vessels to preserve heat and protect vital organs, then dilates them after the cold exposure, promoting better blood circulation and nutrient delivery.*

• *This cold exposure also stimulates the production of norepinephrine, a hormone that has anti-inflammatory and pain-relieving properties.*

Benefits of Cryotherapy for Longevity:

• **Reduction of Inflammation:** *Cryotherapy helps reduce inflammation, which is a major factor in aging and the development of age-related diseases such as arthritis, cardiovascular disease, and neurodegeneration.*

• **Improved Skin Tone:** *Cold temperatures can boost collagen production, leading to tighter, firmer skin and a reduction in fine lines.*

• **Enhanced Recovery and Performance:** *Cryotherapy can help athletes recover from intense training by reducing muscle soreness and promoting faster tissue repair.*

• **Increased Metabolism and Fat Loss:** *Exposure to cold temperatures increases metabolic rate, which may aid in fat loss over time.*

Practical Use:

• *Cryotherapy is usually done in specialized centers using cryo-chambers or localized devices. Sessions typically last 2-3 minutes, and regular use (2–3 times a week) may be required for optimal benefits.*

3. Nootropics (Cognitive Enhancers)

Nootropics, often referred to as "smart drugs" or "cognitive enhancers," are substances—either natural or synthetic—that are believed to improve brain function, memory, focus, and overall cognitive performance. They have gained attention in the longevity space for their potential to protect the brain from age-related decline and improve mental clarity as we age.

How Nootropics Work:

• *Nootropics work by affecting the brain's neurochemistry, increasing the levels of neurotransmitters like dopamine, serotonin, and acetylcholine, which are involved in mood regulation, memory, and learning.*

• *Some nootropics are believed to increase blood flow to the brain, enhance neuroplasticity (the brain's ability to form new neural connections), and protect against oxidative damage to neurons.*

Popular Nootropics for Longevity:

• **Caffeine + L-Theanine:** *A combination of caffeine (for focus and energy) and L-Theanine (for relaxation and reduced stress) is commonly used for cognitive enhancement.*

• **Rhodiola Rosea:** *An adaptogen that helps manage stress and fatigue, which could be particularly useful in reducing age-related cognitive decline.*

• **Bacopa Monnieri:** *An herb used in traditional medicine to enhance memory, learning, and reduce anxiety.*

• **Lion's Mane Mushroom:** *A natural nootropic that supports brain health by promoting nerve growth factor (NGF), which supports the growth and maintenance of neurons.*

Benefits of Nootropics for Longevity:

• **Cognitive Protection:** *Some nootropics may help delay or reduce the onset of age-related cognitive conditions, such as Alzheimer's and dementia.*

• **Improved Focus and Memory:** *In both young and older adults,* *nootropics may boost short-term memory, focus, and overall brain performance.*

• **Mood Enhancement:** *By increasing levels of neurotransmitters, nootropics can improve mood and reduce symptoms of depression and anxiety, which often increase with age.*

Practical Use:

• *Nootropics can be taken in various forms, such as capsules, powders, or drinks. However, it's important to research individual supplements carefully and consult a healthcare professional before starting a regimen, as effects may vary.*

Balancing Cutting-Edge Methods with Natural Approaches

While biohacking methods like red light therapy, cryotherapy, and nootropics show great potential for longevity, it's crucial to balance these cutting-edge techniques with natural, time-tested approaches to health. The best biohacking strategies combine modern science with traditional wisdom.

1. Prioritize Healthy Lifestyle Habits First

Before diving into advanced biohacking tools, ensure that you are prioritizing foundational longevity practices:

• **Nutrition:** *A nutrient-dense, whole-food diet rich in antioxidants, healthy fats, and anti-inflammatory foods.*

• **Exercise:** *Regular physical activity, including strength training, cardiovascular exercise, and flexibility training.*

• **Sleep:** *Prioritize sleep hygiene to ensure sufficient, restorative sleep every night.*

• **Stress Management:** *Incorporate relaxation techniques like mindfulness, yoga, or meditation to combat chronic stress.*

These practices form the foundation of longevity and will amplify the effects of biohacking tools.

2. Personalized Approach to Biohacking

Not all biohacking methods will work for everyone, and individual responses can vary. It's essential to consider your own health goals, preferences, and any existing health conditions before embarking on a biohacking regimen. A personalized approach may include:

• **Consulting with a healthcare professional** *before starting biohacking practices, particularly for more advanced techniques.*

• **Tracking biomarkers:** *Use tools like wearables or blood tests to track health metrics (such as heart rate variability, inflammation, and metabolic markers) to assess the impact of biohacking methods on your body.*

• **Experimenting with different approaches:** *Trying a combination of biohacking techniques and evaluating what works best for your body and mind.*

3. Avoiding Over-reliance on Technology

While biohacking tools can be beneficial, they should not replace foundational habits. For example, relying solely on nootropics to boost cognitive function without adequate sleep, physical exercise, and nutrition is unlikely to provide long-term benefits. Similarly, using cryotherapy without addressing underlying stress or inflammation may not offer lasting results.

Biohacking should complement—and not replace—natural practices that support overall health and wellness.

The Future of Biohacking and Longevity

Biohacking is a rapidly evolving field that holds tremendous promise for those seeking to optimize their health and extend their lifespan. Tools like red light therapy, cryotherapy, and nootropics offer exciting possibilities for enhancing physical and cognitive health. However, for these methods to be effective and sustainable, they must be combined with holistic, natural approaches to wellness, including nutrition, exercise, and stress management.

By integrating cutting-edge biohacking techniques with time-tested longevity practices, you can create a comprehensive, personalized approach to living a longer, healthier life. As the science of biohacking continues to evolve, we can expect even more innovative tools to emerge, but the core principles of health and longevity will remain grounded in the fundamentals of self-care and balance.

CHAPTER 25
THE FUTURE OF ANTI-AGING MEDICINE

The field of anti-aging medicine has evolved significantly over the past few decades. With advances in regenerative medicine, genetic engineering, and cutting-edge technology, the future holds exciting possibilities for slowing, halting, and even reversing some aspects of aging. As researchers continue to explore ways to extend lifespan and improve healthspan, the potential for breakthroughs in anti-aging medicine grows ever more promising. However, with these advancements come important ethical considerations that need to be addressed as we push the boundaries of science and longevity. This chapter will explore the future of anti-aging medicine, focusing on the latest advancements in regenerative medicine, aging research, and the ethical implications of these innovations.

Advances in Regenerative Medicine and Aging Research

Regenerative medicine and aging research are two of the most rapidly advancing areas of science today. Together, they offer the potential to repair or replace damaged tissues, promote cellular regeneration, and slow the aging process. Here are some of the most exciting breakthroughs and trends shaping the future of anti-aging medicine:

1. Stem Cell Therapy

Stem cell therapy holds enormous promise for regenerative medicine. Stem cells are undifferentiated cells that have the ability to become any type of cell in the body. As we age, our bodies' ability to regenerate and repair tissues diminishes, but stem cells can potentially restore this capacity.

How Stem Cell Therapy Works:

• **Cell Replacement and Repair:** *Stem cells can be injected into damaged tissues, where they can differentiate into the necessary cell type and promote healing. For example, in joint degeneration, stem cells can be used to regenerate cartilage.*

• **Tissue Regeneration:** *Stem cells may also be used to regenerate organs and tissues that have aged or become dysfunctional, including the skin, heart, liver, and even neurons in the brain.*

Current and Future Applications:

• *Stem cell therapy is already being used in some clinical trials to treat diseases like osteoarthritis, heart disease, and neurological conditions. In the future, stem cell-based therapies may help to repair tissues damaged by aging and extend lifespan by enhancing the body's natural regenerative processes.*

2. Telomere Extension and Telomerase Activation

Telomeres are protective caps at the ends of chromosomes that shorten each time a cell divides. As we age, telomeres become progressively shorter, leading to cellular aging and the eventual death of cells. Telomerase is an enzyme that can lengthen telomeres, potentially reversing the effects of aging at the cellular level.

How Telomere Therapy Works:

• **Telomerase Activation:** *Telomerase can be artificially activated or introduced into the body to lengthen telomeres, theoretically allowing cells* *to divide for a longer period before becoming senescent (aging or dysfunctional cells).*

• **Potential Impact on Aging:** *By extending the life of cells, telomere extension could delay the onset of age-related diseases, such as cardiovascular disease, neurodegeneration, and immune system decline.*

Current and Future Applications:

• *Research is ongoing to develop telomere-lengthening therapies, including gene therapy, small molecules, and enzyme activation. While these approaches are still in the experimental stage, they represent one of the most exciting avenues in anti-aging medicine.*

3. Senescence Cell Clearance (Senolytics)

Senescence refers to a state where cells no longer divide and become dysfunctional. These "senescent" cells accumulate with age and contribute to inflammation, tissue dysfunction, and age-related diseases. Senolytics are drugs or compounds designed to target and remove senescent cells, potentially reversing some of the damage caused by aging.

How Senolytics Work:

• **Clearing Senescent Cells:** *Senolytics work by inducing apoptosis (programmed cell death) in senescent cells, which can reduce inflammation and promote the regeneration of healthy tissues.*

• **Promoting Healthier Aging:** *By removing senescent cells, senolytics could slow the progression of age-related conditions such as arthritis, heart disease, diabetes, and cognitive decline.*

Current and Future Applications:

• *Early clinical trials have shown that senolytic drugs may improve physical function and reduce symptoms of aging. As research progresses, senolytics could become a key part of anti-aging therapies aimed at enhancing healthspan and preventing age-related diseases.*

4. Gene Editing and Genetic Reprogramming

Gene editing technologies, such as CRISPR, allow for precise modifications of the DNA in living organisms. In the context of aging, gene editing could be used to reverse genetic damage, repair defective genes, and enhance the body's ability to resist aging.

How Gene Editing Works:

• **Repairing Genetic Damage:** *Gene editing could correct genetic mutations that contribute to aging, improve the body's ability to repair damaged DNA, and even turn back the clock on cellular age.*

• **Reprogramming Cells:** *Scientists are exploring ways to "reprogram" adult cells into more youthful, pluripotent cells, similar to stem cells, which have the potential to regenerate damaged tissues and organs.*

Current and Future Applications:

• *Gene editing is still in its infancy when it comes to aging-related applications, but early research holds great promise. The potential to use gene editing to correct genetic defects or even reverse aging processes could redefine what it means to age.*

Ethical Considerations in Anti-Aging Medicine

While the advances in anti-aging medicine are thrilling, they also raise significant ethical questions that need to be addressed. The power to extend lifespan and slow aging could have far-reaching implications on society, healthcare, and the environment. Below are some of the primary ethical considerations that need to be explored as we move forward with anti-aging technologies:

1. Access and Equity

One of the most pressing ethical concerns is the potential inequality in access to these technologies. Advanced treatments like stem cell therapy, gene editing, and telomere extension are likely to be expensive and may only be available to a small portion of the population. This raises the issue of who will benefit from these technologies and whether they will create a greater divide between the wealthy and those who cannot afford them.

Considerations:

• *Will access to life-extending therapies be limited to those with economic resources, creating a world where longevity is determined by wealth?*

• *How can governments and policymakers ensure that advancements in anti-aging medicine are accessible to a broader population?*

2. Overpopulation and Environmental Impact

Extending human lifespan could result in a significant increase in the global population, leading to potential issues with overpopulation, resource scarcity, and environmental strain. While advancements in longevity may offer individuals more years of healthy living, they could also place greater pressure on the planet's ecosystems and infrastructure.

Considerations:

• *How will societies accommodate an aging population with increased life expectancy? Will there be enough resources to support longer lifespans?*

• *Could these advances contribute to unsustainable population growth, particularly in regions where life expectancy is already high?*

3. The Nature of Aging and Human Identity

The ability to slow or reverse aging could challenge our fundamental understanding of what it means to age and live a human life. If we are able to extend life significantly, the concept of a "natural" lifespan may change, leading to philosophical and existential questions about the purpose and meaning of life.

Considerations:

• *What does it mean for an individual to live for centuries? How will extended lifespans affect our identities, relationships, and life goals?*

• Will we lose the sense of urgency that comes with a finite lifespan, potentially impacting motivation and personal growth?

4. Consent and Safety in Experimental Therapies

As with any cutting-edge technology, the safety and efficacy of anti-aging treatments must be thoroughly tested before being made available to the public. Gene therapies, stem cell treatments, and senolytics are still in the early stages of development, and long-term side effects are not fully understood. The question of whether individuals can fully consent to experimental treatments with potentially unknown outcomes is critical.

Considerations:

• Are patients fully informed of the potential risks when undergoing experimental anti-aging therapies?

• How can we ensure that these treatments are safe and ethical before being used widely?

The Future of Anti-Aging Medicine and Its Ethical Balance

The future of anti-aging medicine holds great promise, with advances in regenerative therapies, gene editing, and cellular reprogramming offering unprecedented opportunities to extend healthy lifespan. Technologies like stem cell therapy, telomere extension, senolytics, and nootropics could revolutionize our approach to aging, slowing or even reversing the biological processes associated with getting older.

However, these advancements must be carefully balanced with ethical considerations that address issues of access, overpopulation, environmental impact, and personal identity. As we move forward, it is crucial to ensure that these powerful technologies are developed and implemented in a way that promotes equality, safety, and sustainability.

In the coming decades, anti-aging medicine may transform the way we age and redefine our understanding of life itself. As we navigate these exciting possibilities, we must remain mindful of the ethical implications that accompany the ability to extend life and delay aging. The future of aging may be brighter than ever, but it requires careful thought, responsibility, and an ethical approach to ensure that its benefits are felt by all.

CHAPTER 26

BUILDING YOUR PERSONAL LONGEVITY PLAN

In your journey toward a longer, healthier life, creating a personalized longevity plan is essential. While general principles of nutrition, exercise, and wellness apply to everyone, each person's needs, goals, and challenges are unique. A well-crafted, individualized plan will not only increase your chances of living longer but also ensure you enjoy optimal health and vitality throughout your life. This chapter will guide you through the steps of setting up your personalized longevity plan, focusing on goal setting, tracking progress, and customizing key areas such as nutrition, exercise, and daily habits.

1. Setting Goals and Tracking Progress

A successful longevity plan begins with clear, measurable goals. Establishing long-term objectives will help you stay motivated, while tracking your progress ensures you're moving in the right direction. To build a lasting plan, focus on SMART goals—goals that are Specific, Measurable, Achievable, Relevant, and Time-bound. This structured approach will not only make your goals actionable but also allow you to measure your success over time.

Setting Longevity Goals

· **Health Goals**: Set goals that relate to key aspects of longevity, such as improving your cardiovascular health, boosting immune function, or enhancing brain health. For instance, you might aim to lower your cholesterol or blood pressure to within an optimal range or improve your cognitive function by engaging in activities that boost memory.

· **Fitness Goals**: Develop goals that target your physical strength, flexibility, endurance, and mobility. This might include walking 10,000 steps a day, practicing yoga three times a week, or incorporating weightlifting into your routine for muscle maintenance.

· **Dietary Goals**: Nutrition plays a critical role in longevity. Set specific dietary goals, such as increasing your daily intake of vegetables and fruits, cutting back on processed foods, or following a balanced eating schedule.

· **Mindset and Mental Health Goals**: Longevity isn't just about physical health—mental well-being is just as important. Set goals to practice mindfulness daily, work on stress reduction, or cultivate positive thinking through daily gratitude practices.

Tracking Your Progress

· **Health Metrics**: Regularly track your key biomarkers, including blood pressure, blood sugar, cholesterol, and weight. Use wearable devices like fitness trackers or smartwatches to monitor physical activity, heart rate, sleep quality, and more.

· **Journaling**: Keep a daily or weekly journal to track your habits, including meals, workouts, sleep, and mood. Journaling can help you identify patterns and adjust your plan accordingly.

· **Self-Assessment**: At regular intervals, review your goals to assess whether you're meeting them. Make adjustments to your plan as needed, but ensure you stay realistic and flexible with your approach.

· · ·

2. Customizing Your Longevity Blueprint: Nutrition

Nutrition plays a central role in longevity, and customizing your diet to suit your specific needs is key. Depending on factors such as age, health conditions, activity levels, and personal preferences, you may need to fine-tune your dietary choices to optimize your health and longevity.

Personalized Nutrition Tips

· **Macronutrient Balance**: Ensure you're consuming the right balance of carbohydrates, proteins, and fats. A Mediterranean-style diet, rich in fruits, vegetables, whole grains, lean proteins, and healthy fats, is widely associated with longevity. For those who are physically active, ensure you're getting enough protein to support muscle maintenance and repair.

· **Anti-Inflammatory Foods**: Focus on foods that fight inflammation, such as berries, leafy greens, nuts, seeds, turmeric, and fatty fish rich in omega-3s. Chronic inflammation is a significant contributor to age-related diseases, so reducing it through diet can have a profound impact on your healthspan.

· **Calorie Moderation**: While calorie restriction is not the only key to longevity, eating in moderation and avoiding overeating is essential. Practice mindful eating by listening to your body's hunger cues, and consider implementing strategies like intermittent fasting to promote cellular repair and longevity.

· **Personalized Supplements**: While whole foods should be your primary source of nutrition, certain supplements may benefit your specific needs. Speak with a healthcare provider to determine if additional supplementation, such as vitamin D, omega-3 fatty acids, or probiotics, could benefit your health based on your current state of health.

3. Customizing Your Longevity Blueprint: Exercise

Physical activity is one of the most important pillars of longevity. Regular exercise helps maintain muscle mass, bone density, cardiovascular health, flexibility, and mental clarity. However, the type and intensity of exercise you choose should be tailored to your personal needs, preferences, and goals.

Personalized Exercise Strategies

· **Strength Training**: As we age, we naturally lose muscle mass and strength. To counteract this, incorporate strength training into your routine, focusing on exercises that work all major muscle groups. Aim for two to three strength training sessions per week, using free weights, resistance bands, or bodyweight exercises.

· **Cardiovascular Exercise**: Engaging in regular aerobic activity is essential for heart health and longevity. You might choose to walk, jog, cycle, swim, or practice any form of aerobic exercise you enjoy. Aim for at least 150 minutes of moderate-intensity exercise or 75 minutes of vigorous-intensity activity each week.

· **Flexibility and Balance**: Maintaining flexibility and balance is crucial for preventing falls and improving overall mobility. Yoga, Pilates, and tai chi are excellent ways to improve flexibility, balance, and mindfulness. These practices can also help reduce stress and enhance relaxation.

· **Non-Exercise Movement**: In addition to structured exercise, focus on non-exercise physical activity throughout the day. This includes walking, standing, stretching, or engaging in hobbies like gardening or dancing. The more movement you incorporate into your daily routine, the better.

4. Customizing Your Longevity Blueprint: Daily Habits

The small daily habits you practice can have a profound impact on your longevity. These habits work together to promote overall well-being, reduce stress, and ensure that you stay on track with your goals.

Mindfulness and Stress Reduction

Stress is one of the greatest contributors to aging and disease. Developing a routine that includes mindfulness, meditation, or deep breathing exercises can help reduce stress and improve mental clarity. Consider incorporating practices like:

• **Mindful breathing** *for a few minutes every morning or during breaks throughout the day*

• **Gratitude journaling** *to foster positive thinking*

• **Meditation or yoga** *to calm the mind and improve emotional well-being*

Sleep Optimization

Quality sleep is essential for recovery, cellular repair, and overall longevity. Customize your sleep routine by:

• **Creating a sleep-friendly environment***: Ensure your bedroom is dark, quiet, and cool.*

• **Establishing a consistent sleep schedule***: Go to bed and wake up at the same time every day, even on weekends.*

• **Limiting screen time** *before bed to ensure you're winding down properly.*

Building Social Connections

Strong relationships and social connections contribute to emotional health and longevity. Invest in nurturing relationships with family, friends, and community members. You might consider:

• *Regularly connecting with loved ones*

• *Participating in group activities, such as volunteering or taking classes*

• *Cultivating deep, supportive friendships that foster a sense of belonging and well-being*

5. Revising and Evolving Your Longevity Plan

A personalized longevity plan is a dynamic, evolving document. Your goals, needs, and preferences will change over time, and so should your plan. Regularly evaluate your progress and make adjustments as necessary. Whether it's tweaking your diet, changing your workout routine, or exploring new stress-reduction techniques, continual adaptation is key to maintaining a plan that works for you.

A Blueprint for Lifelong Health

Your personalized longevity plan is a roadmap for living a longer, healthier life. By setting clear goals, tracking progress, and tailoring your nutrition, exercise, and daily habits, you can ensure that you're making choices that support your long-term health and vitality. Remember, longevity is not just about adding years to your life, but about adding life to your years. Through intentional planning and mindful living, you can build a future that is not only longer but also richer in health, happiness, and fulfillment.

CHAPTER 27
DAILY HABITS FOR LIFELONG WELLNESS

Achieving longevity and optimal health isn't just about occasional big changes—it's about the daily habits that compound over time to create a foundation for lifelong wellness. By establishing a sustainable routine that incorporates small, intentional habits, you can maintain energy, vitality, and overall health well into old age. This chapter will explore the daily habits you can adopt to enhance your life, as well as morning and evening practices that promote longevity and overall well-being.

1. Establishing a Sustainable Routine

The key to long-term success in health and longevity lies in consistency. A sustainable routine should incorporate habits that are realistic and enjoyable, making them easier to maintain for years. Your routine should support your goals for longevity while also enhancing your quality of life. Below are the foundational components of a wellness routine that can be customized to fit your unique needs.

Morning Rituals to Start Your Day Right

Your morning sets the tone for the entire day. Starting your day with practices that energize and ground you can make a big difference in your overall health and longevity.

· **Wake Up Early**: Rising early gives you time to center yourself, reduces stress, and allows you to begin the day with intention. Aim to wake up at the same time every day, even on weekends, to regulate your circadian rhythm.

· **Hydrate Immediately**: After several hours of sleep, your body is dehydrated. Start your day by drinking a glass of water to help rehydrate and jumpstart your metabolism.

· **Mindfulness or Meditation**: Spend a few minutes practicing mindfulness or meditation. Focusing on your breath or reflecting on gratitude can help reduce stress and set a positive, calm tone for your day.

· **Light Movement or Stretching**: Gentle stretching or light movement, such as yoga or a short walk, can help increase circulation, improve flexibility, and reduce the stiffness that can come from sleep. This is a great way to awaken your body and prepare it for the day ahead.

· **Healthy Breakfast**: A nutritious breakfast sets the stage for balanced energy throughout the day. Include protein, healthy fats, and fiber-rich carbohydrates to stabilize your blood sugar levels and avoid energy crashes.

Midday Practices for Sustained Energy

To keep your energy levels high and avoid burnout during the day, it's important to incorporate habits that nourish your body and mind throughout the afternoon.

· **Take Breaks**: Make sure to take breaks during your workday to stretch, walk, or meditate. Taking a few minutes every hour to stand and move will reduce the risk of muscle strain, promote circulation, and prevent mental fatigue.

· **Lunch That Fuels You**: Aim for a balanced, nutrient-dense lunch with whole foods. Incorporate lean proteins, healthy fats, and plenty of vegetables to maintain your energy. Avoid overeating, as large meals can leave you feeling sluggish in the afternoon.

· **Move More**: Stay active throughout the day, even if it's just a brisk 10-minute walk after meals. This supports digestion, increases circulation, and keeps your metabolism active.

Evening Rituals to Wind Down and Promote Restful Sleep

The evening is just as important as the morning in your wellness routine. How you end your day can significantly impact the quality of your sleep and your overall well-being.

· **Eat a Light, Nutrient-Rich Dinner**: A heavy dinner late at night can disrupt sleep and digestion. Opt for a lighter dinner that includes vegetables, lean protein, and healthy fats. Avoid eating too close to bedtime to give your digestive system time to process food before sleep.

· **Limit Screen Time**: The blue light emitted from screens (phones, tablets, computers) interferes with the production of melatonin, the hormone that regulates sleep. Try to turn off electronics at least an hour before bedtime to help your body transition into sleep mode.

· **Evening Meditation or Reflection**: Practice mindfulness in the evening to reflect on your day and release any lingering stress. A guided meditation or breathing exercises can help you unwind and prepare your mind for restful sleep.

· **Prepare for Sleep**: Develop a wind-down ritual that signals to your body that it's time for sleep. This might include a warm bath or shower, reading a book, or practicing relaxation techniques. Keep your bedroom cool, dark, and quiet to create an optimal sleep environment.

· **Sleep Consistency**: Aim to go to bed at the same time each night to support your circadian rhythm. Sleep is critical for rejuvenating the body, repairing tissues, and maintaining cognitive function.

2. The Power of Small, Consistent Habits

The key to maintaining a routine for lifelong wellness is ensuring that your daily habits are small and manageable. Instead of trying to overhaul your entire lifestyle overnight, make gradual changes that become second nature. These habits can add up over time, leading to significant improvements in your health and longevity.

Physical Activity Habits

· **Daily Movement**: Aim to move every day, whether it's a walk, stretching, or a more intense workout. Even just 30 minutes of light exercise each day can support cardiovascular health, increase strength, and boost your mood.

· **Non-Exercise Physical Activity**: Incorporate more movement throughout your day, such as standing while talking on the phone, taking the stairs, or doing household chores. These small actions can help improve circulation and combat the negative effects of a sedentary lifestyle.

Nutrition Habits

· **Eat Mindfully**: Practice mindful eating by paying attention to how food makes you feel. Avoid distractions (like eating in front of a screen) and focus on savoring your meals. This habit helps with digestion, prevents overeating, and encourages a healthier relationship with food.

· **Snack Wisely**: If you're hungry between meals, choose snacks that support your health, such as nuts, seeds, fruits, or veggies. Avoid processed or sugary snacks, which can cause energy crashes and contribute to inflammation.

· **Meal Prep**: Consider preparing meals in advance to ensure that you always have healthy options available. This eliminates the temptation of unhealthy takeout or fast food and makes it easier to stick to a nutritious diet.

Mindset and Stress Management Habits

· **Gratitude Practice**: Take a few minutes each day to write down or reflect on things you're grateful for. Practicing gratitude has been shown to improve mental health, increase optimism, and reduce stress.

· **Breathing Exercises**: Incorporate short breathing exercises throughout your day to lower stress levels and improve focus. Simple practices like deep diaphragmatic breathing or box breathing can calm your nervous system and increase relaxation.

· **Positive Affirmations**: Develop a habit of using positive affirmations to boost your confidence and mindset. Repeat affirmations each morning or during moments of stress to help shift your focus toward positivity and resilience.

3. Staying Flexible and Adapting Your Routine

While consistency is crucial for creating lasting change, it's also important to stay flexible. Life is full of unexpected events and changes, and your routine should adapt to these shifts. If you miss a day of exercise or don't get enough sleep one night, don't be discouraged. Focus on getting back on track the next day and be compassionate with yourself.

Adapting Your Routine Based on Needs

· **Seasonal Changes**: Your wellness routine may need to shift with the seasons. In the winter, you might focus more on indoor activities, while in the summer, you can spend more time outdoors. Adjusting your routine to the environment can make it more enjoyable and sustainable.

· **Life Events**: During stressful periods—whether it's a big project at work or a personal challenge—your routine might need to be adjusted. Don't sacrifice sleep or nutrition during these times, but try to incorporate shorter, less intense workouts or mindfulness practices to maintain balance.

Reevaluating Your Goals and Habits

• **Regular Check-Ins**: *Every few months, revisit your health goals and assess your progress. This will help you determine what's working and where adjustments are needed. Celebrate your successes and make changes to your routine as you learn more about your body and mind.*

The Lifelong Wellness Journey

Building a daily routine that supports longevity is an ongoing, evolving process. By adopting small, sustainable habits that support your physical, mental, and emotional well-being, you're laying the groundwork for a long, healthy life. Whether it's morning rituals that energize you, evening practices that relax you, or the power of consistent, intentional actions throughout your day, these habits will serve as the foundation for a wellness-focused life.

Remember, wellness is not an all-or-nothing endeavor—it's about finding balance and embracing progress, not perfection. With a commitment to daily habits that nourish your mind, body, and spirit, you can create a lifestyle that promotes lifelong vitality and well-being. The journey may be long, but each small step you take toward wellness will be a powerful contribution to your longevity.

CHAPTER 28
LEARNING FROM THE WORLD'S LONGEVITY HOTSPOTS

Across the globe, there are regions known for their extraordinary populations of centenarians—people who live not only longer but healthier lives. These areas are referred to as "Blue Zones," and they offer invaluable insights into the lifestyle habits, diets, and cultural practices that promote longevity. By studying these regions, we can uncover the secrets to living longer and healthier lives. In this chapter, we will explore the lessons learned from some of the world's most famous longevity hotspots: Okinawa, Sardinia, Nicoya, and other regions—and how you can adopt their best practices to enhance your own longevity.

1. The Blue Zones: A Global Perspective

The concept of Blue Zones refers to five distinct regions in the world where people live measurably longer, healthier lives. These regions include Okinawa (Japan), Sardinia (Italy), Nicoya Peninsula (Costa Rica), Ikaria (Greece), and Loma Linda (California, USA). Researchers have studied these areas to identify common factors contributing to the residents' long, healthy lives. While each region has its own unique cultural and environmental characteristics, there are several overarching lifestyle practices that link them together.

2. Okinawa, Japan: The Island of Immortals

Okinawa, often dubbed the "Island of Immortals," is home to one of the highest concentrations of centenarians in the world. Okinawans have long been studied for their longevity, with many people living past 100 while remaining active, mentally sharp, and in good health.

Key Lessons from Okinawa

· **Plant-Based Diet**: The Okinawan diet is primarily plant-based, consisting of vegetables, tofu, sweet potatoes, and small portions of fish and lean meats. This diet is rich in antioxidants and anti-inflammatory foods that protect against aging and disease.

· **Hara Hachi Bu**: One of the most well-known habits of Okinawans is the practice of "Hara Hachi Bu," which means eating until you are 80% full. By avoiding overeating, they reduce the risk of obesity and related diseases such as diabetes and heart disease.

· **Strong Social Connections**: Okinawans place great value on relationships and community. They have a network of close friends called "moai," a group of people who provide emotional support and social connection throughout life. This sense of belonging and purpose has been linked to improved mental and physical health.

· **Physical Activity**: Okinawans remain physically active throughout their lives, whether it's through gardening, walking, or traditional activities like Tai Chi. Daily movement is a central part of their lifestyle, contributing to physical health and emotional well-being.

3. Sardinia, Italy: The Mountainous Land of Centenarians

Sardinia, particularly the highland areas, has one of the highest concentrations of centenarians in the world. The rugged terrain and tight-knit communities have contributed to the longevity of its residents. Sardinians live well into their 90s and 100s, enjoying an active, social, and purpose-filled life.

Key Lessons from Sardinia

· **Wine and Heart Health**: While the Sardinian diet includes a moderate amount of wine, it's consumed in small quantities with meals and is often red wine, rich in antioxidants. The polyphenols in wine, especially resveratrol, are thought to promote heart health.

· **Mediterranean Diet**: The Sardinian diet is rich in whole grains, vegetables, beans, and olive oil, which are staples of the Mediterranean diet. Sardinians also eat small portions of meat, primarily from goats and sheep, which provide lean protein. This diet has been linked to lower rates of cardiovascular disease and cancer.

· **Daily Movement and Livelihood**: Much like Okinawans, Sardinians remain active throughout their lives. Many elders still walk for miles every day, climb hills, and tend to their gardens or animals. The physical activity embedded in daily life, rather than formal exercise routines, is a key factor in their longevity.

· **Sense of Family and Purpose**: Sardinians place a strong emphasis on family and intergenerational support. Older individuals are often integrated into family life, providing a sense of purpose and mental engagement. This connection to family and culture is vital for emotional and mental well-being.

4. Nicoya Peninsula, Costa Rica: A Longevity Hotspot in Central America

The Nicoya Peninsula in Costa Rica is home to another high concentration of centenarians. Residents of Nicoya live longer and healthier lives due to a combination of diet, lifestyle, and cultural factors. Research suggests that their longevity is also influenced by the region's unique environment, water, and social systems.

Key Lessons from Nicoya

· **The Nicoyan Diet**: The Nicoyan diet is based on whole, unprocessed foods, with beans, corn, and rice as staples. They also consume a significant amount of fruits, such as papayas and oranges, which are rich in vitamins and antioxidants. Nicoyans also include small amounts of animal protein, primarily from local sources like pork and eggs.

· **Hard Work and Physical Activity**: Physical labor is a significant part of life for many Nicoyans, even into old age. Their routine includes work in agriculture, gardening, and other physically demanding tasks. This daily physical activity contributes to maintaining strength and mobility well into advanced age.

· **Strong Family Values and Community**: Like Okinawa and Sardinia, Nicoyans prioritize close family relationships and a sense of community. They often live in extended family households, providing them with emotional support, social engagement, and a sense of purpose.

· **Active, Positive Mindset**: The Nicoyan culture places importance on maintaining a positive outlook on life. Many Nicoyans follow a religious or spiritual practice, which provides them with a sense of meaning and purpose.

5. Ikaria, Greece: The Island of "Happy" Longevity

Ikaria, an island in the Aegean Sea, is known for its high percentage of people over the age of 90 who are active, healthy, and mentally sharp. Ikarians have some of the lowest rates of chronic diseases and dementia in the world, making it another model for longevity.

Key Lessons from Ikaria

· **Mediterranean Diet**: Ikarians follow a Mediterranean-style diet, rich in vegetables, legumes, olive oil, and fish. Their meals are high in fiber and healthy fats, and they enjoy moderate portions of meat and dairy. This nutrient-dense, low-calorie diet helps prevent chronic illnesses and contributes to healthy aging.

· **Social and Relaxed Lifestyle**: In Ikaria, life is slow-paced, and there is little stress. People take time to relax, take afternoon naps, and spend time socializing with friends and family. The combination of social interaction and regular relaxation helps reduce the negative effects of stress on the body.

· **Physical Activity**: Much like other Blue Zones, Ikarians remain physically active throughout their lives, often through walking, gardening, and outdoor activities. Staying physically engaged in daily life helps preserve muscle mass, mobility, and cardiovascular health.

6. Loma Linda, California: The Blue Zone in the U.S.

Loma Linda, California, is home to a large population of Seventh-day Adventists, a religious group that has embraced principles of health and wellness for over 150 years. This community enjoys a significantly longer lifespan than the general U.S. population.

Key Lessons from Loma Linda

· **Plant-Based Diet**: The typical Adventist diet is plant-based, focusing on vegetables, nuts, whole grains, and legumes. Many members also avoid alcohol, caffeine, and processed foods, which may contribute to their extended lifespan.

· **Focus on Faith and Purpose**: A strong sense of faith, community, and purpose is central to the Adventist lifestyle. The belief in the importance of family, spiritual practices, and social service provides meaning and contributes to both mental and physical health.

· **Regular Exercise and Rest**: Adventists prioritize both exercise and rest. Regular physical activity, such as walking, hiking, or swimming, is an integral part of their routine. They also prioritize getting adequate sleep, which is crucial for overall health and longevity.

7. Adopting Blue Zone Best Practices

To adopt the best practices from these longevity hotspots, consider the following strategies:

· **Adopt a Plant-Based, Whole Food Diet**: Prioritize fruits, vegetables, legumes, whole grains, and healthy fats. Limit processed foods and red meat, and focus on nutrient-dense, anti-inflammatory foods.

· **Practice Hara Hachi Bu**: Eat until you are 80% full, rather than overeating, to prevent weight gain and metabolic diseases.

· **Stay Active**: Incorporate physical activity into your daily routine through walking, gardening, or other activities you enjoy.

· **Cultivate Strong Social Connections**: Build and maintain meaningful relationships with family, friends, and community.

· **Focus on Purpose**: Whether through spiritual practices, hobbies, or community involvement, find a sense of purpose that provides fulfillment and meaning.

· **Prioritize Rest and Relaxation**: Develop habits that reduce stress and ensure adequate sleep. Consider daily mindfulness, meditation, or simply taking time to unwind.

Embracing Global Longevity Wisdom

By learning from the world's longevity hotspots, we can begin to adopt practices that support health and wellness throughout our lives. Whether it's through a nourishing diet, daily physical activity, or fostering strong social connections, the common threads found in these regions are simple yet powerful tools for living a longer, healthier life. While each person's journey is unique, these insights provide a blueprint for longevity that can be adapted and embraced for a life full of vitality and purpose.

CHAPTER 29
FACING CHALLENGES WITH GRACE

Aging is an inevitable part of life, but it doesn't have to be a process filled with fear, resistance, or loss. As we age, we inevitably face challenges—physical limitations, changes in relationships, health concerns, and the loss of loved ones. However, the key to a long and fulfilling life is how we face these challenges. Embracing the aging process with grace and dignity is crucial for maintaining emotional well-being, cultivating resilience, and ensuring a high quality of life in our later years. In this chapter, we will explore how to adapt to life's inevitable changes and age with grace, dignity, and resilience.

1. The Wisdom of Acceptance: Embracing Change

One of the greatest challenges of aging is the inevitable changes that come with it—whether in our bodies, our minds, or our lives. Aging brings shifts in our health, appearance, and sometimes even our social roles. While these changes can be difficult to accept, it is important to recognize that resistance to change often leads to frustration, stress, and unhappiness.

Key Principles of Acceptance:

· **Redefine Aging:** Instead of viewing aging as a loss or decline, embrace it as a new chapter of life filled with opportunities for growth and self-discovery. Aging can bring freedom, wisdom, and the ability to focus on what truly matters.

· **Cultivate Mindfulness:** Practicing mindfulness allows us to live in the present moment without judgment. When we accept the changes that come with aging, we can fully embrace life as it is. By letting go of attachment to past versions of ourselves, we can enjoy each stage of life without feeling the weight of comparison.

· **Self-Compassion:** Be kind to yourself during times of change. Acknowledge the challenges that come with aging and treat yourself with the same compassion you would offer a friend. Aging is not a failure—it is a natural, beautiful part of the human experience.

2. Resilience: Bouncing Back from Setbacks

Resilience is the ability to bounce back from adversity and maintain a sense of well-being despite challenges. As we age, resilience becomes even more important, as we may face health problems, the loss of loved ones, or other life events that shake us. Developing resilience is key to aging gracefully.

Key Components of Resilience:

· **Adaptability:** Being flexible in the face of change allows us to navigate difficult situations with less stress. Embrace a mindset of adaptability, knowing that life's challenges are opportunities for growth.

· **Emotional Regulation:** Resilient individuals are able to manage their emotions in the face of stress. This doesn't mean avoiding negative emotions, but rather acknowledging and processing them in a healthy way. Practices like deep breathing, meditation, or journaling can help regulate emotions and maintain mental balance.

· **Building Support Systems:** Resilience is strengthened by having a strong support system. Surround yourself with positive relationships, whether through family, friends, or community groups. These relationships provide emotional support, encouragement, and a sense of belonging.

· **Self-Efficacy:** Cultivate a belief in your ability to handle life's challenges. When we feel competent and empowered, we are better able to navigate difficult times and emerge stronger.

3. Aging with Dignity: Preserving Self-Respect

Aging with dignity means maintaining a sense of self-respect and autonomy, regardless of physical or mental changes. It involves continuing to live with purpose, engaging in activities that bring joy, and being proactive about health and well-being.

Key Principles of Aging with Dignity:

· **Maintain Autonomy:** As we age, it's important to preserve our independence as much as possible. Simple practices, like staying physically active, making decisions about our health care, and maintaining social connections, help retain our autonomy.

· **Prioritize Health and Well-Being:** Aging gracefully means taking care of our bodies, minds, and spirits. Regular exercise, a balanced diet, and stress management are key to maintaining vitality and self-respect. Similarly, taking time for self-care and nurturing mental health through practices like meditation or therapy can help preserve dignity.

· **Stay Engaged in Life:** People who age with dignity are often those who remain engaged with life. Continue to pursue passions, hobbies, and new interests. Lifelong learning, whether through reading, learning a new skill, or joining a new social group, fosters a sense of purpose and keeps the mind sharp.

· **Seek Meaningful Connections:** Relationships are at the core of dignity in aging. Maintaining strong, supportive connections with family, friends, and community helps prevent isolation and loneliness, which can have detrimental effects on both mental and physical health.

4. Finding Purpose in the Later Years

A strong sense of purpose is one of the most significant contributors to aging with grace. Research has shown that people who have a sense of purpose live longer, healthier lives. In later years, finding meaning and purpose in daily activities can improve mental and physical health, help manage stress, and increase overall happiness.

Ways to Find Purpose:

· **Mentorship and Teaching:** Sharing your wisdom and experience with others is a powerful way to create purpose. Whether through mentoring younger generations or volunteering in your community, teaching others fosters a sense of legacy and contribution.

· **Creative Pursuits:** Engaging in creative activities like writing, painting, music, or crafts can provide both personal fulfillment and a sense of purpose. These activities allow you to express yourself, stay mentally active, and create something meaningful.

· **Community Involvement:** Many people find purpose through involvement in their community. Whether it's participating in social organizations, volunteering, or taking part in religious or spiritual practices, helping others and being part of a group gives life meaning.

5. Overcoming the Fear of Aging

The fear of aging is common, often fueled by societal pressures, unrealistic beauty standards, and the fear of losing independence or vitality. However, confronting and overcoming this fear is essential to aging with grace.

Confronting Aging with Courage:

· **Reframe Aging as a Gift:** Instead of fearing aging, view it as a privilege. Not everyone has the opportunity to grow old, and each day adds richness to our lives. Embrace the unique experiences that come with each age and stage.

· **Cultivate Gratitude:** Practicing gratitude for the present moment and the experiences of life can shift the focus from fear to appreciation. Acknowledge the strengths and wisdom you've gained over time, and be thankful for your body's resilience.

· **Accept Impermanence:** Aging is a reminder of the impermanence of life. Learning to accept this reality helps reduce the fear of aging and encourages us to live more fully in the present.

6. End-of-Life Planning: Preparing with Grace

While it can be difficult to think about, preparing for the end of life is a part of aging with dignity. Thoughtful end-of-life planning can alleviate stress for loved ones and ensure that your wishes are respected. This process can also bring peace of mind and allow for a graceful transition.

Key Steps in End-of-Life Planning:

· **Advance Directives:** Clearly outline your wishes for medical care in case you are unable to make decisions for yourself. This can include decisions about life support, organ donation, and pain management.

· **Create a Will:** Ensure that your assets and personal belongings are distributed according to your wishes. This can alleviate stress for your family and prevent legal complications.

· **Open Conversations with Loved Ones:** Having open and honest conversations about your wishes for end-of-life care and funeral arrangements ensures that everyone is on the same page and can help ease the burden on your loved ones.

Aging with Grace and Purpose

Aging is a journey that presents both challenges and opportunities. Facing life's changes with grace means embracing the process of aging with acceptance, resilience, and dignity. By adapting to changes, maintaining strong relationships, cultivating purpose, and preparing for the future, we can navigate the aging process in a way that enriches our lives and preserves our sense of self-respect. Aging with grace allows us to live each stage of life to its fullest, and with dignity, we can approach the future with confidence, knowing we've lived a life well-lived.

CHAPTER 30
LIVING FULLY EVERY DAY

The secret to a long and fulfilling life isn't just about longevity —it's about living fully in every moment. While it's important to focus on our health, longevity practices, and the big-picture approach to life, the real magic happens when we learn to savor the present. Living fully means immersing ourselves in each day with intention, purpose, and an appreciation for the beauty that surrounds us. It's not enough to simply exist for many years; the true key to a long life is finding joy in every step of the journey. In this chapter, we will explore how to cultivate presence and make every moment count, ensuring that you not only live longer but live better.

1. The Art of Presence: Living in the Now

Presence—the ability to truly be in the moment—is one of the greatest gifts you can give yourself. Too often, we find ourselves preoccupied with the past or future, which prevents us from fully appreciating the present. Whether it's a conversation with a loved one, a walk in nature, or enjoying a meal, the ability to be fully engaged in the present moment enhances the quality of life and helps us embrace the joys of everyday living.

How to Cultivate Presence:

· **Mindfulness Practices:** Engage in mindfulness meditation or breathing exercises that focus your attention on the present. This practice can help quiet the mind and reduce stress, allowing you to be fully immersed in the moment.

· **Engage Your Senses:** When you are doing an activity, pay attention to the details. Notice the colors, sounds, smells, and textures around you. This helps ground you in the present and can make everyday experiences feel more vibrant and meaningful.

· **Let Go of Multitasking:** Multitasking may seem efficient, but it often diminishes the quality of your experiences. Instead, focus on one task at a time, giving it your full attention. Whether it's cooking, exercising, or having a conversation, being present in the moment increases your satisfaction and enjoyment.

· **Practice Gratitude:** One of the simplest ways to stay present is to focus on what you are thankful for in the moment. Gratitude shifts your perspective, helping you appreciate life's simple pleasures.

2. Savoring Life's Simple Pleasures

Living fully means finding joy in the small moments. In a world that constantly pushes for more—more success, more wealth, more experiences—it can be easy to overlook the simple joys that make life beautiful. Savoring life's pleasures isn't about accumulating possessions or achievements; it's about taking the time to appreciate what already exists around you.

Ways to Savor Life:

· **Slow Down and Enjoy the Moment:** Take time to engage in activities that allow you to savor the experience. Whether it's enjoying a cup of tea, watching a sunset, or having a deep conversation with a friend, don't rush through these moments. Let them unfold slowly and fully.

· **Be Playful:** Playfulness is a form of presence, allowing us to experience joy without the weight of responsibilities. Find time to engage in activities that make you laugh, feel light-hearted, and reconnect with your inner child.

· **Nourish Your Body and Soul:** Truly savoring life also means nourishing yourself with healthy food, ample rest, and positive influences. The more we take care of ourselves physically, emotionally, and spiritually, the more we can enjoy each day.

· **Embrace Nature:** Nature has a way of grounding us and helping us feel connected to the present moment. Whether it's a walk through the woods, sitting by the ocean, or simply spending time in a garden, nature offers an unparalleled sense of peace and beauty.

3. Making Every Moment Count

Life is fleeting, and every moment offers an opportunity to live more fully. To make every moment count, it's essential to live with intention. While it's easy to get caught up in the rush of daily tasks and obligations, true fulfillment comes from being mindful of how we spend our time and energy.

Key Strategies for Making Every Moment Count:

· **Align Actions with Values:** Reflect on your values and let them guide your decisions. When you live according to what truly matters to you—whether it's family, creativity, kindness, or adventure—you create a life filled with meaning.

· **Practice Self-Compassion:** Recognize that it's okay to have moments of imperfection. Living fully isn't about perfection—it's about embracing life's ups and downs and being kind to yourself through all of it.

· **Set Intentional Goals:** Make sure your goals are aligned with your passions and aspirations. Rather than just going through the motions, set clear intentions that reflect the life you want to create.

Break these goals down into small, achievable steps that keep you motivated and present.

· **Be Grateful for Each Day:** At the end of each day, reflect on the moments that brought you joy or gratitude. Whether it was a small achievement or a simple pleasure, acknowledging these moments helps you recognize that every day holds value.

4. Embracing Challenges as Opportunities

Life is not always easy, and the inevitable challenges that come our way can sometimes feel overwhelming. However, how we approach these challenges determines whether they become setbacks or opportunities for growth. To live fully, we must learn to view challenges as a natural part of the process of life, and an opportunity for transformation.

Turning Challenges into Opportunities:

· **Reframe Setbacks:** Rather than viewing challenges as obstacles, try reframing them as learning opportunities. Each difficulty provides a chance to develop resilience, problem-solving skills, and strength.

· **Stay Positive:** Embrace an optimistic mindset, even when faced with adversity. Research has shown that positive thinking is linked to longer, healthier lives. Optimism helps reduce stress and promotes a greater sense of well-being.

· **Practice Flexibility:** Life rarely goes exactly as planned. Being adaptable allows you to flow with life's changes, rather than resisting them. The more flexible you are, the more easily you can navigate life's ups and downs while maintaining a sense of fulfillment.

· **Stay Connected:** During difficult times, maintaining strong relationships can provide emotional support and perspective. Stay connected with loved ones and community groups, and lean on them when you need encouragement.

5. Living a Life of Legacy

Living fully is also about leaving behind a legacy that reflects your values and the impact you want to make on the world. A legacy doesn't have to be monumental or grandiose; it can be small acts of kindness, love, and compassion that ripple outward to those around you.

Ways to Build a Legacy:

· **Teach and Inspire:** Share your knowledge and experiences with others, whether through mentorship, writing, or simply being a role model. Your legacy lives on through the lessons you pass down.

· **Contribute to a Cause:** Get involved in causes that align with your values. Whether it's volunteering, donating, or advocating for change, your contributions can leave a lasting impact on the world.

· **Cultivate Meaningful Relationships:** The connections you build throughout your life are one of the most important aspects of your legacy. Invest in relationships that bring joy, support, and love, and leave a legacy of kindness and generosity.

Living Fully Every Day

The key to longevity and vitality isn't just about living longer; it's about living better. Every moment offers an opportunity to live more fully, to savor life's experiences, and to make a positive impact on those around us. By cultivating presence, embracing challenges, and living with intention, we can make every day count. Ultimately, living fully every day means embracing life with gratitude, purpose, and an openness to the richness of each experience. This mindset not only enhances the quality of our years but also makes the journey of aging something to be celebrated.

Live fully, live with purpose, and make each moment a meaningful step in your ongoing journey of growth and fulfillment.

CHAPTER 31

CONCLUSION: THE BLUEPRINT FOR A LONGER, HEALTHIER LIFE

As we've explored throughout this book, the path to a longer, healthier life isn't found in a single magic solution, but rather in a holistic approach that incorporates nutrition, lifestyle habits, mindset, and the relationships we cultivate. It's a blueprint —a collection of principles that, when embraced consistently, can help you live not only longer but better.

Each chapter has provided a piece of the puzzle, from the power of purpose and positive thinking to the importance of physical activity, sleep, and mindful eating. You've learned the science behind longevity, how to personalize your approach to health, and the importance of building resilience in the face of life's inevitable challenges.

Tying the Blueprint Together

All of these elements work together as part of a larger system designed to enhance both your lifespan and healthspan. It's about nurturing every aspect of your well-being—physical, mental, emotional, and social—while continually adapting to life's changes with grace and purpose.

The foundation of this blueprint is built on the understanding that longevity is not about merely adding years to your life; it's about adding life to your years. It's about living with intention, savoring the present, and nurturing yourself and those around you in meaningful ways. Through small daily actions, you can create a life that supports vitality and longevity.

Encouragement to Take the First Step Today

The most important step is the first one. You don't need to implement every piece of this blueprint at once—just take one small action today that aligns with the life you want to create. Whether it's making a healthier food choice, starting a mindfulness practice, getting outside for a walk, or reaching out to connect with someone you love, every positive decision you make adds up over time.

Remember, you don't need to be perfect. Life is a journey, and every small effort counts. The key is consistency and a mindset of growth. As you take one step today, know that you are shaping your future self in ways that will benefit you for years to come.

In closing, this blueprint is not just a set of guidelines; it's a philosophy for living a fulfilling, vibrant life—one that is marked by purpose, connection, joy, and health. So, take that first step today, embrace the process, and trust that every moment lived with intention brings you closer to a longer, healthier, and more meaningful life.

Here's to your journey—a life lived fully, in mind, body, and spirit. The path to longevity begins now.

ELO MARC